SPIRITUAL RENEWAL IN YOUR FAMILY

SPIRITUAL RENEWAL IN YOUR FAMILY

A Fresh Encounter With God in Your Home

HUBERT L. SEALS

Foreword by David Ferguson

Pathway PRESS

Library of Congress Catalog Card Number: 99-070449
ISBN: 0-87148-992-9

Copyright © 1999 by Pathway Press
Cleveland, Tennessee 37311
All Rights Reserved
Printed in the United States of America

DEDICATION

- To my wife, Kathy, my best friend, faithful fan, and the love of my life. The question is asked in the book of Proverbs, "An excellent wife who can find?" I DID!

- To my mother, Beatrice, whose prayers and godly example have been the greatest spiritual influence in my life.

- To my children—Lee, Sylvia, and Amber—who bring joy into my life every day.

CONTENTS

Foreword

Christianity as we know it today cannot survive if we lose the battle for the family! With fresh Biblical insights and practical methods for equipping, my friend Hubert Seals prepares us and our homes for victory, abundance and blessing. Here you will find a comprehensive battle plan to guard your marriage and family from attack, while at the same time experiencing family as God intended.

When our Christian faith is not lived out at home, it soon becomes empty of meaning and irrelevant as a testimony of God's love. In this book, Dr. Seals begins where most other books never even go—to the source of certain victory as husbands, wives and family members live out a fresh encounter with God. Realizing couples and families have limited time and opportunity, this book doesn't waste effort on man-made solutions. It focuses, instead, on developing a lifestyle of living out the Father's heart. By applying it practical, Christ-centered principles, you will experience a depth of intimacy not known since the Garden of Eden when God announced to the first family, "It is very good."

You are to be commended for entrusting yourself and your family members to the ideas and suggestions laid out in this book. By doing so, you will reap the great reward of spiritual renewal.

—David Ferguson, Director
Intimate Life Ministries

Acknowledgments

This book is certainly not a solo effort. I humbly acknowledge God as my inspiration, my strength and my guide. Even though my name is on the front cover of this book, I am indebted to the following people who helped make it possible:

- To Michelle Thompson for the initial spark of encouragement and godly counsel.

- To the prayer warriors who committed to pray for me every day until the book was finished.

- To Tony Lane, David Griffis, Johnny Childers, Bill George and Pat Bradbury for believing in me and encouraging me to accept the challenge of this project.

- To Reginia Collier who typed the entire manuscript and met grueling deadlines with such a sweet spirit.

- To Gary Riggins whose initial editing and guidance were both comforting and challenging.

- To Bill George and his entire editorial staff for their cooperation.

- To Wanda Griffith, book editor, who deserves a gold medal for her attitude and work ethic.

- To Pat Bradbury and her team in marketing who continue to be such a great blessing to me both personally and professionally.

- To Wayne Slocumb who did a masterful job with the cover design.

- To my mentors David Dehner, H. Bernard Dixon, Bill George and Mitch Maloney, who have shape my life and ministry significantly.

- To the North Cleveland Church of God church family who have been the genesis of my passion for family ministry. I am especially indebted to all of our couples and family ministry leaders.

- A special note of appreciation is also in order for the following individuals who were instruments of encouragement and assistance: Ken Bell, Tom George, John Vining, Tim Staggs, Doug Slocumb, Ron Bell, Glenn Procopio, and Marcus Hand.

- Deep appreciation goes to those who helped shape my approach to family ministry: David Ferguson (Intimate Life Ministries), Dennis Rainey (Family Life Ministries), Steve Farrar (Men's Leadership Ministries) and Donald S. Whitney, author of *Spiritual Disciplines for the Christian Life.*

- Lee, Sylvia, and Amber Seals have my vote for best kids in the world. They were so understanding as Dad wrote "The Book."

- My wife, Kathy, is my MVP for the entire writing project. Actually, she is the Most Valuable Player in all areas of my life.

Introduction

Families come in all shapes and sizes—couples with young children, couples with older children, couples with no children, single-parent families, parents whose children have left home (empty nesters). All have the potential to become strong, spiritually healthy families.

War has been declared on marriages and families. We need to strengthen our foundations to withstand the violent earthquakes of this sinful day. Spiritual renewal is the place to start building that foundation.

This book is centered on the belief that, as people of God, we can experience a fresh encounter with Him (vertical relationship) that will powerfully and dramatically affect every family relationship (horizontal relationships).

Today, people are hungry for a deeper walk with God, to experience Him in a fresh way in their families. I believe God is birthing a new and exciting spiritual revival in the hearts of husbands, wives, moms, dads and children. As God revives and renews each family member individually (vertically), all family relationships (horizontally) will be spiritually ignited.

Throughout this book, I emphasize the concept that as we grow closer to God, we automatically grow closer to family members. A genuine renewal in God's Spirit dramatically affects everyone around us—especially those in our family.

I remember my first week on the Lee University campus in 1973. While visiting a local bookstore, I purchased a little plastic set of praying hands that were supposed to glow in the dark. Later that night in my dorm room, I turned out the lights and jumped in bed. No glowing! I was disappointed. A few nights later on one of those rare occasions when I was studying, I had the praying hands right under my study lamp. At bedtime, I flipped off the light and climbed to the top bunk. Out of the corner of my eye I noticed something glowing. It was the praying hands. As I lay there watching the glow slowly dim, I realized that's how it is with our relationship with God. Only when we spend time with Him can we begin to know and reflect His presence in our lives.

The glow of the praying hands eventually dimmed. The only way to rekindle the glow was to put the hands back under the light. We too must be close to the Light of the World in order to glow with His Spirit.

The challenges within the pages of this book have become my personal agenda for life and the spiritual growth plan for my family.

Join me in answering the call to experience spiritual renewal.

Part I

LAYING A SPIRITUAL FOUNDATION

A rock solid spiritual foundation is a prerequisite for spiritual renewal in your family. And *you* can be the catalyst! Beware, however, of trying to build on a faulty foundation. A lifestyle of repentance and obedience is required to lay the foundation for spiritual renewal.

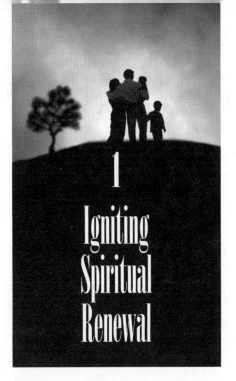

1
Igniting Spiritual Renewal

The big city has certain allure. The next time you find yourself in one of America's major cities, stop and admire the steel and glass that seem to literally scrape the bottom of the sky. Try to locate a construction site where a new high rise is going up. The jackhammers, overhead cranes and huge machinery will be announcing that something big . . . really big . . . is under construction. Look at the sign that has a beautiful picture of this architectural Goliath going up. As you get closer to the fence around the site, you will notice that the clamor, cables and commotion are at least two or three stories below the street, as workmen seem to drill toward China. All of this activity will seem to be in opposition to the picture on the sign. There is no great hole in the ground on the picture—all you will see is what is above ground. Engineers will explain that the building site must first be excavated.

All the loose gravel and dirt must be removed to

expose a solid rock foundation. Then, pillars that support the mammoth structure must be embedded in the bedrock. Eventually the elements (natural or otherwise) will test this most crucial stage of construction. The building stands or falls on the quality of work never seen by the casual observer. Those of us who marvel at how high the building reaches are unaware of the depth of the foundation, even though it is critical to the stability of the building.

Many say that the Leaning Tower of Pisa in Italy is going to fall. Every year scientists measure the building's slow descent. They report that the 179-foot tower moves about one-twentieth of an inch a year and is now 17 feet out of plumb. They further estimate that by the year 2007, the 810-year-old tower will lean too far and collapse onto a nearby restaurant. The word *pisa* means "marshy land" — a clue as to why the tower began to lean even before it was completed. Also, its foundation is only 10 feet deep!

If we are interested in building a solid foundation for our family — a foundation that will withstand the inevitable winds of change — we must take note.

This foundation for spiritual renewal begins with a close relationship with God. "Unless the Lord builds the house, they labor in vain who build it; unless the Lord guards the city, the watchman keeps awake in vain" (Psalm 127:1, *NASB*).

The psalmist does not imply that we do not play a part in building our home. It simply warns us against the futility of leaving God out of the plans. Even with God as our source and strength, we have a responsibility to perform.

I'm reminded of the story of the little girl who

was told to go out on the back porch and bring in her boots. It was already dark, so she was afraid. She failed to persuade her mom, dad and brother to get them because they all agreed that she should go by herself to overcome her fear. They encouraged her, telling her she shouldn't be afraid because God was out there. Finally, the little girl peeped her head out the door and said, "God, since You're already out there, will You throw me my boots?"

It's a cute story, but I don't believe God is in the habit of doing for us what we can do for ourselves. He will help us with our family problems and challenges, but He also expects us to do our part.

In a video series called *Seeking Solid Ground*, John Trent tells of a man whose walls developed cracks in them. He had a contractor repair the cracks, but a few months later, more cracks appeared in his walls. This time he sought the advice of a different contractor, who evaluated the situation and told the homeowner he didn't have a crack-in-the-wall problem; he had a foundation problem. This may also be true of the problems in our relationships with family members. Foundational to building a strong family is for all members to have a strong, spiritual walk with God.

The following diagram depicts this process:

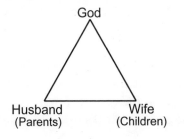

Look carefully at the triangle. Do you see the distance between the husband and wife at the bottom of the triangle? Also, do you see the distance between the parents and children at the bottom of the triangle? Now slowly move up both sides of the triangle toward God. The closer the husband and wife get to God, the closer they automatically get to each other. Also, as parents and children get close to God, they become closer to each other. This has tremendous spiritual potential for family relationships.

Look again at the distance between the husband and wife at the base of the triangle. As they move up the sides of the triangle toward each other, they also get closer to God. As parents and children move up the sides of the triangle toward each other, they too get closer to God. God created the institutions of marriage and family and abundantly blesses those who cherish and honor them. The key to spiritual renewal is a closer relationship with God.

We must strive to be Christlike by walking in the Spirit if we want to lead our families in spiritual renewal. You cannot be the a godly spouse, parent or child if you are not walking in the Spirit.

How can we successfully walk in the Spirit and lead our families to do the same? The following three scriptures give us insight into this challenging opportunity:

> But I keep under my body, and bring it into subjection: lest that by any means, when I have preached to others, I myself should be a castaway (1 Corinthians 9:27, KJV).

> For the sinful nature desires what is contrary
> to the Spirit, and the Spirit what is contrary
> to the sinful nature. They are in conflict with
> each other, so that you do not do what you
> want (Galatians 5:17).

> The one who sows to please his sinful nature,
> from that nature will reap destruction; the one
> who sows to please the Spirit, from the Spirit
> will reap eternal life (Galatians 6:8).

What are you hearing in these verses? Feed the flesh and reap corruption; feed the Spirit and reap life. There are two natures within each Christian, the flesh and the Spirit, and they are at war with each other. Paul, in 1 Corinthians 9:27, was so convinced about the importance of feeding the Spirit he made it a point to keep his body under subjection daily, lest he himself—a man who wrote over half of the New Testament—should become a "castaway." What a graphic picture! The way to walk in the Spirit is to sow to the Spirit, not the flesh.

The question then arises: What are the results of sowing and feeding the Spirit? The works of the Spirit are manifested in "love, joy, peace, patience, kindness, goodness, faithfulness, gentleness and self-control" (Galatians 5:22, 23). Think about it! How much would these Christlike characteristics impact the relationships in your family?

In his book *Spiritual Renewal*, Lamar Vest writes:

> Too many Christians have had their passion
> for things of God dulled by a lust for the

> secular. The things they see, touch, drive or
> put in the bank have come to mean more to
> them than the things of God. The Bible says of
> ancient Judah, "[They made no] difference
> between the holy and the profane" (Ezekiel
> 44:23). We must have a revival of the sacred.
> We must place greater emphasis on pleasing
> God than on fulfilling our own ambitions.[1]

A daily preoccupation of feeding our flesh, at the expense of walking in the Spirit, not only hinders our walk in the Spirit, but it also weakens our influence in our relationship with our families.

We must nourish our spirit, walk in His Spirit and practice Christlikeness. Here are four ways that I believe could revolutionize your relationship with God and your family. (These will be explored more in chapters 4, 5 and 6.)

1. Read God's Word privately and with your family daily.

2. Spend time with God in prayer and lead your family in prayer daily.

3. Lead your family in worship and praise of some kind daily.

4. Look for an opportunity to serve others on a regular basis and encourage each family member to do the same.

If we nourish our spirit in this way every day, we will walk in His Spirit, live in His presence and experience a holy anointing like never before. And remember, it is impossible to give to our spouses or children what we do not possess ourselves. Our personal relationship with God forms the spiritual foundation for our family on which our attitudes, actions, virtues and values are built.

Spiritual Growth

James makes it clear that who we *are* will be manifested in the way we *talk* and the way we *act* (2:18). He says, "I will show you my faith by what I do." We cannot create righteousness, because our righteousness is as filthy rags. Salvation comes by faith in the Son of the living God. However, if we are saved by faith, there will be tangible evidence — good works, kind words and a Christlike attitude. Genuine faith inevitably produces good deeds. This is what spiritual maturity is all about. Warren Wiersbe states it like this:

> Spiritual maturity is one of the greatest needs in churches today. Too many churches are a playpen for babies instead of workshops for adults. The members are not mature enough to eat the solid spiritual food that they need, so they have to fed on milk (Hebrews 5:11-14).

Just look at the problems James dealt with and you can see that each of them is characteristic of little children:

- Impatience in difficulties — 1:1-4.

- Talking but not living the truth — 2:14-26.

- No control of the tongue — 3:14.

- Fighting and coveting — 4:1-12.

- Collecting material toys — 5:1-5.

After over a quarter century of ministry, I am convinced that spiritual immaturity is the number one problem in our churches. God is looking for mature men and women to carry on His work, and sometimes all He can find are little children who cannot even get along with each other.[2]

We need a balance between being and doing. Who we are in Christ is reflected by what we say and what we do. As we endeavor to grow closer to God and mature in Him, we automatically strengthen the relationships in our home, which brings about spiritual renewal.

KEEPING GOD CENTRAL

If we fail to keep God at the center of our lives, our efforts toward strengthening our marriage and family will be severely limited. Everything in our lives hinges upon obeying the Word of God:

> Hear, O Israel: The Lord our God, the Lord is one. Love the Lord your God with all your heart and with all your soul and with all your strength. These commandments that I give

you today are to be upon your hearts. Impress
them on your children. Talk about them when
you sit at home and when you walk along the
road, when you lie down and when you get
up. Tie them as symbols on your hands and
bind them on your foreheads. Write them on
the doorframes of your houses and on your
gates (Deuteronomy 6:4-9).

The Christian family is under attack on every
side, faced with a daily barrage of damaging influences. The forces of evil are at work trying to
destroy families. But our families can remain strong
in the midst of the storms. We can have peace and
joy if we keep God at the center of our home. Even
if we are unable to remove the painful circumstances that our families face, we can still have joy
and peace in the presence of God. Living a life
empowered by the Spirit ensures that our families
will not only survive—they will thrive!

The Battle Is Winnable!

A prominent theme of our day is revival. Today,
God is drawing people to Himself and to each
other, and He wants to begin that work in the two
institutions He created even before the church—the
institutions of marriage and family.

In Genesis 1, God created everything and "it was
good." Then we hear God say that something was
not good. It was "not good that man should be
alone" (2:18). When God created Eve, He created the

first human relationship — marriage. When Cain was born to Adam and Eve, God's creative hand worked in the second human relationship — the family. These relationships are still important in the eyes of God. Our churches, for the most part, are made up of families. Whether they are single-parent families, blended families, couples with no children, couples with children, couples with grandchildren, and so forth, the church consists of people who are living in one or both of the first two relationships God created.

Recently while listening to a Christian radio station, I heard Dennis Rainey talk about a survey that showed the number one thing parents needed help with today in their families is spiritual development.

Another study involving 100 of the happiest families in America showed similar results. Strong families have many components, and experts are not in complete agreement on the relative importance, or ranking, of these components.

Foolproof formulas for successful family life are nonexistent. However, certain themes are prevalent among healthy families: reliance on common senses, teaching through example, give-and-take communication, and the will to discipline. One prominent theme that has emerged is spirituality — believing in a Creator and living by His guidelines. Nearly 90 percent of the families surveyed pointed to spirituality as a significant, if not dominant, guiding force in their lives. Although the words varied — faith, religious beliefs, Christian principles, moral foundation, church family — the idea was the same. Spirituality is the umbrella which encompasses and fosters a more loving, close-knit family.[3]

In today's society, the family itself has been redefined. In virtually any church and community you will find the following:

- Traditional homes with a husband and wife raising children together

- Divorced men and women who have remarried and created a new family unit

- Widows and widowers who have remarried and have blended their families

- Separated mothers and fathers who try to spend an equal amount of time with their children as they sort out their marriage

- Divorced, single parents who are struggling to raise their children without the ongoing presence of a second parent in the home

- Divorced women and men who have returned home to live with their parents, who are working to assist in raising their children.[4]

Each of the above situations can be defined as "family." This book is not written for just one stereotypical, traditional family structure. Whether married, single, a parent or grandparent, the principles of spiritual renewal for the home are applicable. The good news is that we can begin with the family we have, declare it to be a family after God's own heart, and then do everything to bring about spiritual renewal.

We all become frustrated, guilt-ridden and discouraged at times when we view our family as less than perfect. Do you ever suspect that an evil force is behind the attacks on your marriage and family unity, preventing you from growing closer to God, your spouse, and your children? Guess what? It's true! Scripture warns us: "Be on the alert. Your adversary, the devil, prowls about like a roaring lion, seeking someone to devour" (1 Peter 5:8, *NASB*).

Howard Hendricks, a professor at Dallas Theological Seminary, once said, "We are surrounded by foreign, hostile, and home-shattering influences in our world today. The supportive elements of society no longer feed and shade us. The Christian home must blossom in a field of weeds."[5]

As Steve Farrar puts it, "War has been declared upon the family, on your family and mine. Leading a family through the chaos of American culture is like leading a small patrol through enemy-occupied territory. If you doubt the existence of this war, take a look at the casualty list:

- 50 percent of all first marriages and 70 percent of all second marriages end in divorce.

- Extramarital affairs are rampant.

- Child abuse is out of control.

- Each night, enough teenagers to fill the Rose Bowl, Cotton Bowl, Sugar Bowl, Orange Bowl, Fiesta Bowl and the average Super Bowl will practice prostitution to support drug addiction.

- Crime is rampant and criminals are protected by the courts.

- Every 78 seconds, a teenager in America attempts suicide.

- 66 percent of American high school seniors have used illegal drugs.

- 1 million teenage girls will get pregnant out of wedlock this year.

- 500,000 of those girls will abort their babies.[6]

How close have any of these statistics hit home with you or someone you know? You can keep your marriage and family off the casualty list. You can build a strong, spiritual foundation for your family by recognizing these facts:

1. The Enemy's strategy is to destroy your relationship with God, your relationship with your mate, and your relationship with your children.

2. The spiritual strategy God has to empower you and your family is outlined in this book.

The battle for our family is winnable because "greater is He who is in [us] than he who is in the world" (1 John 4:4, *NASB*).

The "Spark" for Spiritual Renewal

In the book *Spiritual Renewal*, Lamar Vest states:

It is noteworthy that none of the great spiritual awakenings of the past were started by a group of ecclesiastical leaders who called a conference and announced, "Now let's get busy and have a spiritual awakening." Quite contrary to that, spiritual awakenings are ushered in by simple people who get so hungry for a move of God they can't eat, sleep or be content until they experience a fresh, explosive move of God. Our plans and programs may help get us in the right frame of mind and spirit, but they will never bring about renewal. Renewal is a gift of God to desperate, spiritually hungry people.[7]

I will never forget the words of my pastor and spiritual mentor, David Dehner. He explained revival one Sunday by saying, "Just draw an imaginary circle around yourself and then ask God to start revival in that circle." That made such a strong impression on my young, hungry heart. To this day, I still pray this way because I know when God touches me, He touches my family. When God rekindles a revival spark in me, it spills over to my wife and children. When God's Spirit bathes me with His love and power, it has a spiritual impact on my family relationships. Howard Heindricks tells about Richard Baxter's focus on revival in the home:

> Richard Baxter was a great man of God who pastored a wealthy, sophisticated parish. For three years he preached with passion in his heart but saw no visible results. Finally, one

day, he threw himself across the floor in his study and cried out, "O God, You must do something with these people or I'll die!"

He said, "It was as if God spoke to me audibly, 'Baxter, you are working in the wrong place. You're expecting revival to come through the church. Try the home.' "

Richard Baxter spent entire evenings in homes helping parents set up times of family worship with their children. He moved from one home to another. Finally the Spirit of God started to light fires all over that congregation, until they swept through the church and made it the great church it became—and made Baxter a man of godly distinction.

We hear much about revival today, but it is always in connection with the church. I wonder if perhaps God is saying to us, "You're working in the wrong place." Ask God to bring revival in your home.[8]

We need strength and wisdom from God regarding our spiritual walk and that of our family. The Christian family has a wonderful Lord and Savior who loves us, cares for us, and understands our struggle. The Bible says:

Therefore, since we have a great high priest who has gone through the heavens, Jesus the Son of God, let us hold firmly to the faith we

profess. For we do not have a high priest who
is unable to sympathize with our weaknesses,
but we have one who has been tempted in
every way, just as we are—yet was without
sin. Let us then approach the throne of grace
with confidence, so that we may receive
mercy and find grace to help us in our time of
need (Hebrews 4:14-16).

We are also exhorted in 1 Peter 5:7 to cast all of our
cares on Him, because He cares for us. There are
three basic steps in beginning the revolutionary
process of igniting spiritual renewal in your family:

1. Desire a strong relationship with God.

2. Develop a lifestyle of repentance and obedience to help ignite spiritual renewal.

3. Depend on God to help you.

I'm sure you've heard these lyrics from an old
song: "It only takes a spark to get a fire going."
Igniting spiritual renewal begins with just a
spark—just one person . . . just you! God can use
you to start the fire of a fresh encounter with Him
in your family. It all begins with you!

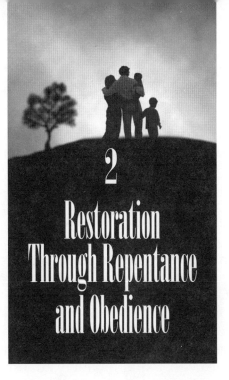

2
Restoration Through Repentance and Obedience

World War II was over. A fleet of U.S. ships was sailing proudly home. The sailor on watch saw a light in the distance. The bridge had him send this message: "Alter your course 10 percent north." The light in the distance returned a message, "Alter your course 10 percent south." The sailor was instructed to send another message, "Alter your course; this is an order." The message returned, "Alter your course; this is a suggestion."

An enraged captain gave the next message to the sailor: "Alter your course; this is a command from an admiral." The response came back, "Alter your course; this is a seaman third class speaking."

With fury, the captain sent out his final message: "Alter your course . . . this is a battleship." Then came a final response from across the water, "This is a lighthouse . . . it's your call."[1]

Like this sea captain, we may need to take a hard look at the direction our family is traveling. Are we traveling the course of obedience to God's Word? It may be lifesaving for us to reassess our individual spiritual walk with God and the spiritual climate in our home. In this quest for spiritual renewal in our family, turning from destructive family patterns is crucial. We must then turn toward God in obedience—following His rules for right relationships. Ed Cole suggested, "You cannot gain through sacrifice what you lose through disobedience." God is looking for men and women who will live in obedience to His Word and His will. There will be no doubt about the spiritual climate in a home where God is honored and obeyed. God will permeate that kind of family atmosphere and renew the heart of every family member.

Repentance Begins With You

Spiritual renewal begins first in the heart. It will not begin in a series of revival services, or in a wave of evangelism. It must begin with personal repentance. This is how we draw closer to God. As we move closer to God we get closer to our mate and children.

In Westminster Abbey, these words can be found on the crypt of an Anglican bishop who died around the year 1100:

> When I was young and free and my imagination had no limits, I dreamed of changing the world. As I grew older and wiser, I discovered the world would not change, so I shortened my sights somewhat and decided to

change only my country. But it, too, seemed immovable. As I grew into my twilight years, in one last desperate attempt, I settled for changing only my family, those closest to me, but alas, they would have not of it. And now as I lie on my deathbed, I suddenly realize: If I had only changed myself first, then by example I would have changed my family.[2]

A related principle comes from John Maxwell: "If you want to change an organization, change the leader. If you want to change a church, change the pastor. And if you want to change a family, change the parents."[3] Spiritual growth and renewal begins at the top and is always preceded by personal repentance.

The prophet Ezra demonstrated his need for personal repentance as he confessed his own sins and turned to God on behalf of the priests and people.

> Now when Ezra had prayed, and when he had confessed, weeping and casting himself down before the house of God, there assembled unto him out of Israel a very great congregation of men and women and children: for the people wept very sore. . . . And they made proclamation throughout Judah and Jerusalem . . . that they should gather themselves together unto Jerusalem. . . . And Ezra the priest stood up, and said unto them, Ye have transgressed. . . . Now therefore make confession unto the Lord God of your fathers,

and do his pleasure: and separate yourselves
from the people of the land. . . . Then all the
congregation answered and said with a loud
voice, As thou hast said, so must we do (Ezra
10:1, 7, 10-12, KJV).

Spiritual renewal is a first-person matter. Dennis
Rainey experienced this with his Family Life staff as
they discussed the concept of family reformation.

Early one morning, I stood before a small
group of men at our Family Life office in
Little Rock. I had invited them to discuss the
concept of Family Reformation. I had no idea
a different kind of housecleaning was about
to begin . . . in my house.

On the chalkboard, in large letters, someone
had written the words "Family Reformation."
We talked about those two words and what it
would take for a family reformation to occur
in America. We identified the needs of families. Observations bantered back and forth
like balls in a tennis match. A stream of ideas
poured forth. We were hopeful and optimistic. But an hour into our discussion, the
tone of the meeting changed dramatically.
Staring at the chalkboard, each of us, one by
one, fell silent. Instead of dreaming about all
things that must occur "out there" in the culture, we gradually realized something had to
happen "in here" and "in us" first. A daunt-
ing question had silenced us: "Lord, what

needs to change in my life for a family reformation to occur in my home?" Not much else
was written on the chalkboard.   Instead of
crafting a resounding battle cry for the mass-
es, we ended up with individual introspec-
tion, earnest prayers, and somber hearts.
What does God expect of me? The meeting
adjourned early.[4]

Spiritual renewal begins with repentance, and
repentance begins with you. Wherever you are in
your relationship with God and your family, start
there. You cannot undo the past any more than you
can unscramble eggs.   Furthermore, God doesn't
expect you to. God desires for us to have a dynamic relationship with Him, walking and living in His
Spirit. He also desires that your family enjoy the
same. We are the catalyst, and God will help.

Steps to Repentance

Three basic steps lead to true repentance in
renewing and restoring our relationships with
God, our mate and our children.

1. *We must **choose** truth.* God is displeased with
harsh words, selfish actions, unfaithfulness, anger,
unforgiveness, ungodly behavior, or any other evil
that breaks covenants with Him or our families.
His Word reveals sin and its destructive patterns
in relationships. God holds the plumb line of His
Word to measure our faithfulness in choosing His
commands.

2. *We must* **confess.** True repentance and confession touch the heart of God. This can be seen when contrasting the lives of King Saul and King David. At first glance, the outcome of these Biblical characters seems a bit unfair. Saul partially disobeyed God, and as a result experienced problems the rest of his life, dying a horrible death. On the other hand, after committing adultery and murder, King David ended up living a full and meaningful life, died at a ripe old age, and had it said of him, "He was a man after God's own heart." Now, how can this be? It's almost as if the punishments of Saul and David were switched. David seemed to sin more, but had less punishment. Saul seemed to sin less, but had more punishment. Why? Because of true confession. The issue was not which king sinned the most, but which king truly confessed and dealt with his sin. Just listen to the cry of David's heart:

> Have mercy on me, O God, according to your unfailing love; according to your great compassion blot out my transgressions. Wash away all my iniquity and cleanse me from my sin. For I know my transgressions, and my sin is always before me. Against you, you only, have I sinned and done what is evil in your sight, so that you are proved right when you speak and justified when you judge. . . . Create in me a pure heart, O God, and renew a steadfast spirit within me (Psalm 51:1-4, 10).

Keith Lynch, an associate with *Family Life* broadcast ministry, shared the following story of an incident in his home. Many of us can identify with him as he shares how he had to choose between his own self-determined way or God's way:

> Even as we finished the breakfast rush and got the kids to school, I could feel the tension mounting. I had wronged my wife, Jonell. I watched, somewhat amused, as we circled each other warily. I have developed the fine art of winning the argument at any cost, especially when I am in the wrong! My mind clicked into action as she began to accurately recite the liturgy of my error. As I caught my breath, readying my tongue for the task, something happened. Just at that moment, God did one of those surprising things it seems He loves to do. As I revved up my brain for a great "discussion" (read "argument"), I was suddenly dumbstruck. No words came. I watched her fall silent in turn, as she waited, girding herself for my self-defense. But this time, to our mutual surprise, it didn't come. In place of my impeccable logic, the intricate dissection of detail, five simple words came out of my mouth: "I'm sorry. I was wrong." Jonell smiled, and that smile shouted from the rooftop "You are the most godly man to me, for you love me more than your logic, your process, and your need to win." There were no more words between us. Husband, don't argue with your wife from

a position of authority, or gifting, or power, or capacity. Don't "win" just because you can. Simply apologize.

Repentance and confession may not be easy; they may even be bitter at times, but the fruit is sweet. Husbands and wives forgive each other and discover fresh joy, hope and oneness in their relationships. Children regain loving, attentive parents and are raised to fear God and keep His commandments. The estranged are reconnected . . . the haughty are humbled . . . the guilty find relief and freedom.[5]

These are the kinds of relationships in which spiritual renewal in our families can grow and flourish.

3. *We must **change** our action — change our direction.* If we hurt family members with harsh and unholy words, we must repent and forgive them unselfishly as God commands. True repentance will be known by its fruit. It will be evident by a change in our attitudes and actions:

- It will be seen in growth toward Christlikeness.

- It will be manifested in our relationships in the church.

- It will be manifested in our relationships in the home.

God can take our brokenness and make our lives complete when we are open to change.

TURNING TO GOD IN OBEDIENCE

Obedience is the outward expression of an inward love for God. Obedience and love are like two sides of the same coin. If we truly love God, we will obey Him.

Jesus gave these words of comfort: "For whoever does the will of my Father in heaven is my brother and sister and mother" (Matthew 12:50). He also made it clear that obedience is an indication of a person's relationship with God: "If you love me, you will obey what I command" (John 14:15).

In the next few verses, there is a wonderful blessing promised to those who obey: "And I will ask the Father, and he will give you another Counselor to be with you forever—the Spirit of truth. The world cannot accept him, because it neither sees him nor knows him. But you know him, for he lives with you and will be in you" (vv. 16, 17). In verse 23, Jesus becomes more emphatic: "If anyone loves me, he will obey my teaching. My Father will love him, and we will come to him and make our home with him." What a precious promise! Think about it! The God of the universe is promising to build His house *in* you and me. But the promise is to those who obey.

Earlier we discussed repentance as a change in direction or turning from sin. It follows then that righteousness is in the opposite direction. Obedience is turning *toward* God in attitude and actions. Experts in behavior management suggest that the best way to stop a bad habit is to replace it with a good habit. They also tell us that if we repeat an act for 21 consecutive days, it will become a habit. This concept has positive implications for spiritual disciplines leading to greater godliness.

Nowhere in God's Word do we find the number 21 to be a formula for developing spiritual disciplines. However, the more we repeat something, the more it becomes a habit. As any fourth-grade teacher can tell you, that's exactly the way we learned 9 times 4 equals 36, or that a noun is a person, place or thing. Unfortunately, there is no substitute for rote memory. We all practiced memorization in school and at home. Homework was not necessarily fun, but it was effective.

God's Word tells us, "Do not let any unwholesome talk come out of your mouths, but only what is helpful for building others up according to their needs, that it may benefit those who listen" (Ephesians 4:29). In obedience to that scripture, think how life-changing it would be if husbands or wives began and ended each day with a positive word of affirmation for each other. If that is not already a habit in your life, why not take the "21-Day Challenge" and try it. Say something to "build up" your spouse or children every day. You will be amazed at the results. God will honor and bless those who obey His Word.

Destructive Family Patterns

When the spiritual foundations of family are fractured, God will repair and restore them; but in many cases repairing, restoring and maintaining a relationship with God requires repentance. Fundamental family relationships have a similar pattern. When these relationships begin to break down, it's time to stop traveling in that direction, repent and let God bring healing. When destructive patterns of communication develop with my wife or children — patterns not edifying for them nor pleasing in the sight of God — I ask their forgiveness. Then I pray with them, asking God to help me change this pattern of communication.

REMOVING MODERN IDOLS

The Word of God is clear on the matter of idolatry. God did not hesitate when He commanded, "I am the Lord thy God, which have brought thee out of the land of Egypt, out of the house of bondage. Thou shalt have no other gods before me" (Exodus 20:2, 3, KJV).

Throughout His Word we are given admonition not to let the power of wealth and materialism steer our hearts away from God and our family. As Moses warned the Israelites:

> "Beware lest you forget the Lord your God by not keeping His commandments and His ordinances and His statutes which I am commanding you today; lest, when you have eaten and are satisfied, and have built good houses and lived in them, and when your herds and your flocks multiply, and your silver and gold multiply, and

all that you have multiplies, then your heart
becomes proud, and you forget the Lord
your God. . . . And it shall come about if
you ever forget the Lord your God, and go
after other gods and serve them and worship them, I testify against you today that
you shall surely perish" (Deuteronomy
8:11-14, 19, *NASB*).

Most of us have not made a graven image or
molded a golden calf to worship. However, it is
still possible for us to worship idols as the children
of Israel did. Our idols look different from those
Moses dealt with in the wilderness, but they are
just as hated by God. Martin Luther stated it well:
"Whatever your heart clings to and relies on, that
is your god. Anything you love more than God,
anything you fear more than God, anything you
serve more than God, anything you value more
than God becomes your god."[6]

Adrian Rodgers suggests that idolatry may be
our greatest sin. Jesus declared that the greatest
commandment is to love God with all of our heart
and soul and mind (Matthew 22:37). Idolatry
breaks that first and greatest commandment. This
has such sobering implications for spiritual
renewal in our individual lives and in our family.
When anything becomes an idol, we must
acknowledge it, confess it, and change it. We must
"turn from" it and go the opposite direction. We
must not even allow our blessings from God
become idols in our own home.

The following is a beginning list of modern-day idols:

- *Self.* We live in a generation infected with the disease of "me-itis." Paul warned about this in 2 Timothy 3:2: "People will be lovers of themselves." Having a true servant's heart (putting others first) is a sure antidote for this god.

- *Wealth.* Money may not be evil, but the love of it is (see 1 Timothy 6:10). When greed causes us to compromise in any way—ethically or spiritually—it is a god that displeases God. All our monetary means should be guided by godly stewardship.

- *Family.* Ironically, our family must be kept in proper perspective. We are to love, adore and sacrifice for our family, but we must be certain to place God first.

- *Pleasures.* When Christians become clinically depressed because of the results of a football game, something is wrong. The apostle Paul addresses this issue when he writes that some have become "lovers of pleasures more than lovers of God" (2 Timothy 3:4, KJV). Spiritual renewal begins with repentance, and repentance requires that we have no other gods before Him.[7]

LEAVING AND CLEAVING

We must be obedient to God's Word in every

area of life—especially in the marriage relationship. God has given us rules for right relationships in the home.

The very first command to couples is for a man to leave his family and cleave to his wife:

> "For this reason a man will leave his father and mother and be united to his wife, and they will become one flesh" (Genesis 2:24).

Many couples try to cleave without leaving, which causes marital problems. Leaving is a prerequisite to cleaving. If we want God to bless our marriage, we must live in obedience to His Word by leaving, cleaving and becoming one flesh.

Leaving is the first step that leads to marital intimacy. Once this step is taken, cleaving (becoming one flesh) is then possible. Couples may find it difficult to know where to draw the line when it comes to leaving home. God certainly doesn't mean for couples to sever all ties with parents. Neither does He want them to disregard parents' wisdom and advice. Establishing independence doesn't mean acting in opposition to parental suggestions. If the apron strings are still attached, the process of leaving and cleaving cannot take place. The leaving process forces couples to become more dependent on each other and on God so that their marriage can flourish.

ROLES AND RESPONSIBILITIES

Husbands and wives must take their God-ordained roles and responsibilities in the marriage relationship seriously. The Word of God defines the husband's role as leader and his responsibility to love. The wife's role as helper and her responsibility to submit is also clear.

For years, the feminist movement has blurred the lines between men and women and undermined families in the process. Not only have marriages been weakened, but also many parents who conform to feminist philosophy no longer teach their children the Biblical pattern for husbands and wives. In time, children will pick up this pattern of ungodly role modeling.

Obeying God's rules for right relationships is indispensable for successful family living. Obedience to God always precedes spiritual blessings. The Book of Ephesians describes how we can live a spiritual life in an unspiritual world. This book is neatly divided with three chapters in each half. The first three chapters provide a theological foundation on who we are in Christ—our wealth in Him, our belief. The last three chapters give us the experiential foundation on what we do in Christ—our walk with Him, our behavior. In these last three chapters, we find practical instruction for successful Christian living. And nestled in the middle of this instruction is a "golden nugget" of wise counsel for husbands, wives and children—the family. Ephesians 5:22-25 deals specifically with the roles and responsibilities of husbands and wives:

> Wives, submit to your husbands as to the Lord. For the husband is the head of the wife as Christ is the head of the church, his body,

of which he is the Savior. Now as the church submits to Christ, so also wives should submit to their husbands in everything.

Husbands, love your wives, just as Christ loved the church and gave himself up for her.

1. *Husband's Role and Responsibility*. It is the husband's role to love—sacrificially. His role is servant-leader, not dictator or sole decision-maker. That goes against the grain of his responsibility—to love sacrificially. Howard Hendricks says it this way in his book, *Heaven Help the Home*:

> The husband is to be the head of the home; he is also to be the heart of the home. It is his leadership which provides authority; it is his heart that provides affection. One without the other always leads to distortion. He is to be a leader; he is to be a lover. If the husband is the leader without being a lover, he is an autocratic individual; if he is a lover without being a leader, he will be a sentimentalist. If he has leadership with love, no woman in her right mind resists placing herself willingly and submissively under a man who loves as Christ loved the church.[8]

That's the key to the husband's role as leader. He is to love his wife as Christ loves the church. How did Christ love the church? He gave His life for it! It is interesting that Paul devotes twice as many words to telling husbands to love their wives than he does in telling wives to submit to their husbands.

Before we go too far, let's look at this explosive word, *submission*. In Ephesians 5, the heart of this instruction calls for a mutual submission. This is God's plan:

- The husband submits to his wife's needs.

- The wife submits to her husband's lead.

The one thing that can destroy submitted love is self-love. Ephesians 5:21 says, "Submit to one another out of reverence for Christ." This verse precedes the instruction to husbands and wives in verses 22-33. The pattern calls for mutual submission.

2. *Wife's Role & Responsibility.* The wife's role is to help and submit.

> So the man gave names to all the livestock, the birds of the air and all the beasts of the field. But for Adam no suitable helper was found. So the Lord God caused the man to fall into a deep sleep; and while he was sleeping, he took one of the man's ribs and closed up the place with flesh. Then the Lord God made a woman from the rib he had taken out of the man, and he brought her to the man (Genesis 2:20-22).

Husbands need the support of their wives. It may even become necessary at times when husbands are wrong. That is not to say that wives go along and not offer loving advice. What it does mean is that the wife should show a genuine spirit of caring. The

whole issue of helping and submitting is inseparable.
Where there is a tender submissive spirit, there is also
a desire to help. Submission in reality is not so much
a matter of outward form; it is an inward matter of
the heart. For a wife to just go along with a husband
but hold anger and bitterness in her heart is not in the
spirit of helping and submitting. The sincerity of the
heart is the essence of Scriptural admonition for
wives in helping and submitting. Many times it's not
what is said or done, but how it is said or done. Since
Paul devoted twice as much time in giving instruction to husbands than wives, I will follow suit.

LIVING IN OBEDIENCE AS PARENTS

The following Scripture references are written
for parents:

- Deuteronomy 6:4-9 tells us to teach our
  children to love God and keep His
  commandments.

- Psalm 78:1-7 tells us to teach our children
  about the deeds, wonders' and power of God
  so that they in turn would pass it down to
  future generations.

- Genesis 26:7-11 indicates that our children
  follow our example.

- Exodus 10:2 tells us to teach our children
  about God's power.

- Matthew 18:6-10 tells us about our responsibility to instruct our children in faith.

- 1 Thessalonians 2:7 tells us that mothers should be gentle in caring for their children.

- Ephesians 6:4 admonishes fathers not to exasperate their children. This applies to both moms and dads, but there is a heavier responsibility directed toward fathers.

There is a key scripture that I believe is a guide for Christian parents:

> You are witnesses, and so is God, of how holy, righteous and blameless we were among you who believed. For you know that we dealt with each of you as a father deals with his own children, encouraging, comforting and urging you to live lives worthy of God, who calls you into his kingdom and glory (1 Thessalonians 2:10-12).

This scripture outlines two important ways we can spiritually nurture our children.

First, set a godly example. This is what "living lives worthy of God" (v. 12) is all about. It means living holy, righteous and blameless before our families. One of my favorite poems could be a motto for all parents:

I'd rather see a sermon
  Than hear one any day.
I'd rather one should walk with me
  Than merely show the way.

The eye's a better pupil

And more willing than the ear.
Fine counsel can be confusing,
   But example is always clear.

For I might misunderstand you
   And the high advice you give,
But there is no misunderstanding
   In how you act and how you live.
                              — Anonymous

The Book of Proverbs tells us, "The godly walk with integrity; blessed are their children after them" (20:7, *NLT*). The spiritual walk of parents will have a tremendous impact on children. We need to choose carefully the example we set.

A man and his young son were climbing a mountain. They came to a place where the climbing was difficult and even dangerous. The father stopped to consider which way he should go. He heard the boy behind him say, "Choose the good path, Dad; I'm coming right behind you!"
                              — Unknown

Second, teaching and training children is what the "encouraging, comforting and urging" part of 1 Thessalonians 2:12 is about. The spiritual training of our children is not the church's responsibility — it is the parents'! It's perfectly fine for parents to lean on the church for assistance, help and encouragement in their child's spiritual development, but it is primarily the responsibility of the parents to teach and train their children. It is also their responsibility to seek assistance in a local church.

A very important piece of advice for parents comes from Josh McDowell:

> Rules without relationship equal rebellion—
> either active resistance or passive indifference.
> If you really want to help your child, the most
> important thing for you to do is not to establish
> rules but to build a strong, loving relationship
> with your child.[9]

All our teaching, training, encouraging and urging will be more receptive and fruitful when we establish loving relationships with our children. All of our family relationships are held together with the mortar of repentance and obedience.

> Obey my voice, and I will be your God, and you
> shall be my people. And walk in all the ways that
> I have commanded you, that it may be well with
> you (Jeremiah 7:23).

God will bless families that live a life of repentance and obedience.

Part II

BUILDING WITH SPIRITUAL DISCIPLINES

A home that will stand must be constructed with the right building materials. Time with God in prayer, nourishing your family with the Word, and nurturing a servant's heart in your family are essential spiritual building materials. A family built on these principles will not only survive – it will thrive.

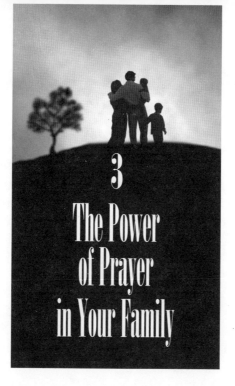

3

The Power of Prayer in Your Family

Several years ago, Mother Teresa spoke on Robert Schuller's television program. Before she spoke, Dr. Schuller reminded her that the program would be aired all over America and in 22 foreign countries. He then asked Mother Teresa if there was one thing that she would like to share with all the viewers. This was her selected response: "Yes, tell them to *pray*. And tell them to teach their children to pray."

Here is a woman whose life was the epitome of good works and sacrificial giving to others. However, when she had to select one message to share with the world, she chose prayer and the importance of teaching children to do the same. In saying so, she suggested that prayer precedes good works. The profound principle at work here is that we as individuals must first touch God if we hope to effectively connect with our spouse and family.

Need for Prayer

Sexual, physical and emotional child abuse has been escalating at an alarming rate. Divorce, infidelity and separations are breaking marriages apart as never before. Children are rebelling against parents and are engaging in drug abuse, illicit sex and violence. We are warned about these conditions in 2 Timothy 3:2-5:

> People will be lovers of themselves, lovers of money, boastful, proud, abusive, disobedient to their parents, ungrateful, unholy, without love, unforgiving, slanderous, without self-control, brutal, not lovers of the good, treacherous, rash, conceited, lovers of pleasure rather than lovers of God—having a form of godliness but denying its power. Have nothing to do with them.

The question is, "Is there hope for our family, our marriage, and our children?" The answer is emphatically, "Yes! There is hope." The answer is clear: "Prayer works"! "The effective, fervent prayer of a righteous man [dad, mother, husband, wife, son, daughter, brother, sister, aunt, uncle, grandparent] avails much" (James 5:16, NKJV).

Jesus' disciples did not ask Him to teach them to sing, preach, organize or lead; they asked Him to teach them to pray. The disciples made the connection between the prayer life of Jesus and the miracle work that typified His life.

Three important spiritual disciplines are necessary

if we are to *be* the kind of spiritual leaders who are leading our families in a walk in the Spirit. The spiritual disciplines of prayer, Bible intake, and service to others (discussed in chapters 3-5) provide the framework that can lead us, and our families, into spiritual renewal. They fuel spiritual growth in our lives. The development of these three spiritual disciplines begins with spending time with God in prayer. In his book *One Home at a Time*, Dennis Rainey, co-founder and executive director of *Family Life*, refers to prayer as an essential home-building material:

> At the risk of sounding simplistic, I believe prayer is the most important factor in healing our families and bring about a family reformation. If this simple discipline were implemented, we would see a stunning difference in our marriages, families, neighborhoods, schools, churches, communities and nation in less than 60 days.
>
> In the 1950s a popular slogan was "The family that prays together stays together." Let's bring that one back! Prayer is the single most important spiritual discipline in every Christian marriage: Husbands and wives must pray together—daily.[1]

Surveys at Family Life marriage conferences indicate that less than 8 percent of all couples pray together on a regular basis. Rainey goes on to say:

> I am not exaggerating when I say that Barbara and I might not still be married had it not

been for daily prayer. In 1972, when we were still just newlyweds, I asked my boss and mentor, Carl Wilson, for his single best advice about marriage. Carl, who had been married to Sarah Jo for 25 years and had four children, said, "Denny, that's easy. Pray daily together. Every night for 25 years we have prayed together as a couple."

An eager, young husband without a clue, I immediately applied Carl's wisdom. Since that day, nearly 25 years ago, Barbara and I have missed daily prayer fewer than a dozen times. That discipline has helped resolve conflicts, kept communications flowing, and most important, acknowledged our utter dependence upon Jesus Christ as the Lord and Builder of our family.[2]

Prayer—A Relationship With God

Prayer is necessary if we are to be who we need to be for our spouse and family. Sometimes we get caught in the trap of spending time working *for* God and not spending very much time *with* God. It is impossible to develop intimacy in any family relationship without spending consistent, quality time with that family member. That same principle is also true with our relationship with God. We must consistently spend time with Him. "Blessed is the man . . . [whose] delight is in the law of the Lord, and on his law he meditates day and night. He is like a tree planted by streams of water. . . . Whatever he does prospers" (Psalm 1:1-3).

For a long time, I viewed prayer as a religious activity that would somehow please God or score points with Him. I viewed it as a duty to perform rather than a relationship to enjoy. Prayer should be a very enjoyable, meaningful and intimate relationship.

Our *concept* of God may determine how we view our *relationship* with God. David Ferguson, president of Intimate Life Ministries, shared a story about his family that made a tremendous impression on the way I view God and my fellowship with Him. He and his wife, Teresa, were sitting in their living room while their newborn grandson, Zachary, slept in the next room. All of a sudden Teresa heard the baby stirring, raced to his bedroom and squealed, "He's awake!" She couldn't wait for him to wake up, so that she could spend time with him. Maybe God feels the same way about us. I would like to think that when I wake up in the mornings, God says, "He's awake! I'm looking forward to spending time with My child today."

Prayer is not something that may lead to a relationship with God. Prayer is enjoying God's presence and relating with Him. Through prayer we experience God's great grace, His loving forgiveness, encouragement for the day and power for the hour.

Exercise of the Soul

There is a strong link between the spiritual discipline of prayer and the Word of God. They go together. A daily balance is critical if we are going to stand strong in the spiritual battle for our family. Paul instructs us: "Train yourself to be godly. For physical training is of some value, but godliness has value for all things, holding promise for both the present life and the life to come" (1 Timothy 4:7, 8).

I like the story Steve Farrar tells about two men who were walking in the woods. Suddenly they see a huge, roaring grizzly bear. Both men know what grizzlies can do. While one of the men sits down and puts on his running shoes, his companion blurts out, "You don't really think you're going to outrun that bear, do you?"

"Of course not," the man replies. "I don't have to. All I have to do is outrun you."[3]

To these two men, endurance became an important issue. Spiritual fitness must be a priority for every family. In his book *Point Man*, Steve Farrar deals with endurance and characterizes prayer as "aerobic kneeling." Here's what he says about prayer and its inseparable relationship with the Word of God:

> Let me ask you a serious question. How do you stay in shape spiritually? If you are going to run the race with endurance and train yourself for godliness, what kind of exercises do you do? In the physical realm you can do aerobic jogging, aerobic basketball, aerobic swimming, aerobic cycling, etc. But in the spiritual realm there is only one such exercise. It's what I call aerobic kneeling. It's also known as prayer.

Prayer is to the soul what exercise is to the body. A spiritual self-starter is a man who is in good spiritual shape. That means he does two things: (1) He consistently eats the nutritious diet of the Scriptures; and (2) he consistently spends time in aerobic kneeling. Prayer is the exercise of the man who is a spiritual self-starter.

These two elements must go together. A marathon runner not only trains efficiently but eats correctly. Both enable him to have physical endurance. The same is true in the Christian life.[4]

It has been my experience that all other spiritual disciplines and Christian graces come from an active prayer life. During times of effective and earnest prayer, God speaks to my heart about other aspects of my Christian and family life:

- My need for confession and repentance
- My need to obey Him in the roles and responsibilities He has given me as a husband
- My stewardship, worship, fasting, evangelism, and any other spiritual discipline
- My need to love my wife and children, sacrificially and unselfishly
- My need to build spiritual traditions that bring my family together and make memories for a lifetime

- My need to live a lifestyle that will leave a godly heritage for my children and grandchildren.

It begins with earnestly seeking God on a daily basis for our own spiritual welfare and for spiritual renewal in our family. Everything else is birthed, nurtured, and grows out of a lifestyle of spending quality time with God in prayer.

Jesus Models Prayer

We should not think of prayer as an impersonal requirement, but a personal joy and privilege. What a privilege to know that the Creator of the universe invites us into His presence to fellowship with Him. "Let us then approach the throne of grace with confidence, so that we may receive mercy and find grace to help us in our time of need" (Hebrews 4:16).

Jesus didn't say *if* you pray . . . He said *when* you pray (Matthew 6:5-7, 9). We must obey His encouragement to see spiritual growth in our own life and renewal in our family.

The call for prayer is not just a call for an occasional trip to our knees when we are in trouble or when we need something. We need to be people of prayer . . . couples of prayer . . . families of prayer. The Bible instructs, "Devote yourselves to prayer" (Colossians 4:2). We need the kind of devotion that requires us to be proactive and to make prayer a priority.

The Key Is Balance

A healthy prayer life will be a balanced prayer life. Some of the basic components of a healthy, balanced prayer life include the following:

- Worshiping, adoring and praising
- Repenting and confessing
- Giving thanks
- Asking
- Interceding

By following this Biblical pattern, we grow spiritually and we bless our families through our prayers beyond the limits of our personal abilities and resources.

Praying For and With Your Spouse

Earlier I mentioned that only about 8 percent of the couples surveyed in Family Life conferences actually prayed together on a regular basis. However, there are very positive results when couples do pray together.

In one study of 600 couples, Dr. James Dobson reported that the couple who prays together and depends on the Bible for solutions to the stresses of living has a distinct advantage over the family with no faith.[5]

In another study, Intimate Life Ministries revealed that only one out of 1014 couples who practice regular devotion times together end up divorcing.[6] Prayer works! It works for marriages and families!

Husbands and wives who commit to consistent prayer times together create a strength that is described as "a cord of three strands [that] is not quickly broken" (Ecclesiastes 4:12). Cecil Myers once said, "Successful marriage is always a triangle: a man, a woman, and God." When God is invited to join a marriage, it will be strong enough to endure. What could be more important than couples praying together? Why then is praying together one of the most challenging practices? It's no secret. Satan knows the power and effectiveness of couples praying together, and he'll do whatever he can to prevent it.

Praying for your spouse touches the heart of God. When I see one of my own children show an act of kindness to another child, I melt. It touches my heart in a tender way. When I hear one of my children praying for another, it touches me deeply. God's heart must be touched in the same way when one of His children (husband, wife or child) prays for another of His children.

We need to pray for our spouses in these areas:

- To know and walk in God's perfect will

- To have joy and peace in their lives

- To be an overcomer in difficult circumstances

- To walk victoriously in the Spirit

- To grow spiritually every day

- To be in health — physically, mentally, emotionally and spiritually

- To be effective in their role and responsibility as husband or wife and as a parent.

Praying *for* your spouse is very important and very effective. Praying *with* your spouse is equally important and can do wonders to create a warmth and tenderness in the marital relationship. Here is a simple prayer that can be modified to help you pray with your spouse:

> Lord, thank You for my husband/wife. I love him/her and I love You for giving him/her to me. Be with him/her at all times. Give him/her peace and joy and keep him/her close to Your heart. Amen.

That is such a simple, yet powerful prayer. Don't shy away from praying with your mate because you feel you have to pray a long formal prayer, or because you feel like you don't have a lot of time. Keep it simple, keep it short, and pray from your heart.

Here is another example of a prayer that Coach McCartney, founder of Promise Keepers, prays with his wife, Lyndi. He kneels beside her, puts his arm around her, and prays something like this:

> Lord Jesus Christ, I invoke Your power and Your Spirit upon Lyndi. Lord, I pray righteousness and purity and holiness upon her. Lord, I pray that You will heal all of her scars,

that You will mend up all those things that keep her from being the woman that she desires to be and that You call her to be.

Lord God, I pray that You will breathe excitement into her, that You will bring about in Lyndi a hope for the future. I pray that I will have favor with her. I pray, Lord, that she will see me and that her heart will rejoice and her spirit will soar when I come in the room.

Lord Jesus Christ, I thank You for this woman. I thank You for the treasure she is, I thank You that she loves You more than me. I pray, Lord, that You will minister to her and that You will build a hedge of protection around her today. Lord Jesus Christ, we need You. All of our hope is in You.[7]

At the close of each day, talk to God together. It's simple. As you lay in each other's arms, express appreciation for one another and to God for allowing you another day to be together. In such simple, intimate times with God and each other, you renew a deep love for God and for each other. Praying like this together brings couples into an intimacy and unity that cannot be achieved any other way.

A national survey on marital satisfaction and happiness discovered that couples who pray together frequently (at least three times per week) have higher levels of marital satisfaction than those who don't.

Dennis Rainey comments on these findings:

> What would happen to the divorce rate in the
> church if husbands and wives would consis-
> tently pray together? I believe that the number
> of divorces could be cut in half within months
> and that within a decade, divorce would be
> uncommon in the Christian community.
>
> If you want to divorce-proof your marriage,
> then make a commitment today to begin
> praying with your spouse.[8]

When husbands and wives pray with one another and bare their souls together with God, there
comes a spiritual renewal and communication that
cannot be achieved any other way. There is no better way to draw closer to God and to each other.

Praying For and With Your Children

Ray Guarendi, in his book *Back to the Family*,
shares the compelling results of a survey of 100 successful families. The author concludes that a fundamental characteristic in successfully raising kids is
to pray for them. Prayer is the supernatural
weapon that empowers and protects your family.[9]
There is an evil raging in our world to sever family
relationships. All our human resources, wisdom
and strength will not be sufficient to win this battle
for our family. "For though we walk in the flesh,
we do not war according to the flesh, for the
weapons of our warfare are not of the flesh, but

divinely powerful for the destruction of fortresses"
(2 Corinthians 10:3, 4, *NASB*).

When we pray for our children, we ally with
God for Him to enter all family situations with His
supernatural wisdom and power. Whether the situation involves rebellion, abuse, drugs, promiscu-
ity, peer pressure, loneliness, important decisions,
relationships, self-esteem or guidance, God is concerned about them all. God is ready to become
supernaturally involved if we will earnestly seek
Him in prayer on behalf of our children. In regard
to his own children, Joe White depicts it this way:

> With a new teenager, I realized all over again
> how the job of parenting was a lot bigger than
> my abilities. That means a lot of prayer.
>
> The Lord says, "You have not because you
> ask not," and "Ask, and you will receive, that
> your joy may be full." I figure that if one
> prayer is good, a thousand would be great. In
> this critical matter of raising teenagers, I want
> to get as close as possible to Paul's directive to
> "pray without ceasing."
>
> We can expect to have Jamie at home for only
> six teenage years. So for six years, I will con-
> centrate in prayer for her . . . asking God to
> make them six golden years.
>
> We ask with faith. God can do it. As Romans
> 8:32 suggests, if God thought enough of us to
> give us His Son, won't He also give us all

things—including the wisdom and strength and love to help her make the most of this season in her life.

So we pray. We pray for all the people in her life: her friends, her teammates, her teachers and coaches, her future husband. We pray for her ability to withstand peer pressure. We pray for her self-image. We pray for her desire to honor and obey us. We pray for our wisdom guiding her. And I pray that the example of my life will be more consistently godly.[10]

Spending time alone with God is one of the greatest gifts that we give to our children. In his book *How to Keep Your Kids on Your Team*, Charles Stanley, senior pastor of the First Baptist Church in Atlanta, tells how his prayer life affected his children:

Many times my children would open my study door and see me stretched out on the floor praying. Most of the time they would close the door quietly and leave. Sometimes, though, Andy or Becky would come in, tiptoe over to where I was, and stretch out beside me. Andy wouldn't say anything, but Becky would wait for a while and then whisper, "Dad, I have a little problem. Could we pray about it together?" I have always believed that two of the most important things I could ever teach them were the importance of prayer and how to pray. I guess the old saying "I'd rather see a sermon than hear one any day" is still true. My children probably could not tell you much of what I have said in sermons on prayer (and I have preached a lot on the subject), but they have both told me that they will never forget seeing me stretched out before God, talking to him about whatever was on my heart. So I know that the best way you can teach your kids to pray is by your example.[11]

John Maxwell, noted author and pastor, writes that we should never underestimate the power and example our prayer life has on our children:

We teach what we know, but we reproduce what we are. Much of what we do today was modeled for us by our parents. For example, without my mother knowing it, I often listened outside my parents' room as she prayed. I learned a lot from that, and it has helped me to be intimate with God in my prayers as an adult.[12]

And lastly, Bill Carmichael, counselor, teacher and author of *7 Habits of a Healthy Home*, tells his story:

It was in the bedroom I shared with my younger brother in our little house on Rutland Avenue in San Jose, California, that I first noticed it. I was seven years old.

I often went to sleep at night hearing my parents talking in the kitchen or laughing with friends in the living room or whispering in their bedroom.

But now, for the first time, I was not just hearing . . . I was listening. I listened to my father praying, "O God, we love you and want you to be the Lord of our lives. We pray for our children, dear Lord." As I listened I heard my name. "And for Billy we pray that you will, even at this age, begin to speak to his heart about following you. We pray that you will give us wisdom in raising this boy. We pray that you will wrap your loving and protecting arms around him and that your heavenly angels will watch over him."

Somehow I knew I was witness to the sacred. I knew this was the Holy of Holies. I knew that what I was hearing was my father's faith, out of the Sunday service and into his everyday life. I knew this was real. His prayer had a profound effect on me. I knew from then on that I was under some kind of special protection and direction. My own spiritual significance began to take on meaning for me from that moment.

Now, forty-five years later, I can still hear the wonderful voice of my father in prayer. I have heard it thousands of times, but I never tire of hearing it again.[13]

Our children learn the importance and power of prayer when we ask them to help us pray about finances, health, church, missionaries, other people's needs and family needs. What could be more gratifying than seeing our children on their knees . . . then seeing the answers to those prayers? I can think of nothing that would help our children's faith grow stronger!

We should take advantage of every opportunity to pray with our children. Mealtimes and bedtimes are naturals. We also need to look for those times when our children are experiencing times of struggle. We also need to rejoice with them in happy times. Offering a prayer of thanksgiving pleases God. It is also good training for the child. We need to be real and conversational with our prayers, just like we're talking to our best friend. This will help our children not to be inhibited about praying, thinking they should pray long and lofty prayers. Look for those opportunities to stop and say to your child, "Would you like for us to pray together about that right now?"

Prayer . . . Just Do It!

Recently, I picked up a bumper sticker in a Christian bookstore that sounded a lot like a familiar Nike tennis shoe commercial. The bumper sticker read, "Prayer—Just Do It!" We can talk about prayer all day long, and even give mental assent to its importance and practice. But until we "do it," prayer cannot affect and empower our families.

Simply saying the word *water* does not make any of us wet. Until we touch it or drink, it has no value. We are still dry and thirsty.

Years ago, I read the painfully honest account Bill Hybels shared about his personal prayer life. It has constantly come back to my mind, and I have shared it both in sermons and seminars. This is what the pastor of America's largest church said in his book *Too Busy Not to Pray*:

> Prayer has not always been my strong suit. For many years, even as senior pastor of a large church, I knew more about prayer than I ever practiced in my own life. I have a racehorse temperament, and the tugs of self-sufficiency and self-reliance are very real to me. I didn't want to get off the fast track long enough to find out what prayer is all about. Several years ago the Holy Spirit gave me a leading so direct that I couldn't ignore it, argue against it or disobey it. The leading was to explore, study and practice prayer until I finally understood it. I obeyed that leading. I read fifteen or twenty major books on prayer, some old and some new. I studied almost every passage on prayer in the Bible. And then I did something absolutely radical: I prayed!"[14]

Godly fathers, mothers, husbands and wives are always fathers, mothers, husbands and wives of prayer. J.C. Ryle said it this way: "What is the reason that some believers are so much brighter and holier than others? I believe the difference, in 19 cases out of 20, arises from different habits about private prayer. I believe that those who are not eminently holy pray little, and those who are eminently holy pray much."[15]

The depth of our prayer life dramatically affects our relationship with our spouse and children. Where there is prayer there is godliness. Spurgeon said it this way: "Even as the moon influences the tides of the sea, even so does prayer . . . influence the tides of godliness."[16]

Dads, moms, husbands, wives, kids—we can't afford *not* to pray! Our spiritual well-being, our marriages and our families are at stake!

4

Nourishing Your Family With the Word

Robert Sumner wrote in his book, *The Wonder of the Word*, about a man who was horribly injured in an explosion. His face was severely disfigured. He lost both hands as well as his eyesight. In addition to his agony and physical pain, he was devastated because he had just recently become a Christian and now he could not read his Bible. Sometime later, this man heard about a woman in England that could read the Braille Bible with her lips. He was excited about the possibility of doing the same. His excitement soon turned to more disappointment; his lips were so severely damaged that he could not feel the characters. However, one day as he was trying to read, his tongue brushed the page and he could feel the characters. He was so elated as he thought, *I can read the Bible using my tongue.* By the time his story had appeared in *The Wonder of the Word* in 1988, the man had read the entire Bible four times with his tongue.[1]

The necessity for spiritual nourishment for our family compels us to find ways to feed on God's Word. When combined with the spiritual discipline of prayer, nothing could be more important to our family's spiritual growth and renewal than God's Word. As we continue to construct the framework of spiritual renewal in our homes, it is critical that we focus on His Word.

GUIDING OUR FAMILY

We cannot live in spiritual health without a constant diet of spiritual food. We will become spiritually depleted if we do not regularly feed on God's Word.

1. *The Word of God anchors our lives.* The purpose of an anchor is to keep a boat from floating into dangerous waters. The Bible anchors us and prevents us from being swept away by every wind of adversity or tidal wave of discouragement. It stabilizes our walk with God and keeps us from drifting into dangerous compromises that can destroy us spiritually.

2. *The Word of God gives direction for our lives.* A friend of mine once told me about an airplane pilot who experienced vertigo. He was in the clouds with zero visibility when he looked at his instrument panel and didn't believe what he saw. Although it felt like he was flying level, his instrument panel indicated that he was flying straight down. He trusted his feelings, and when he came out of the clouds he realized he was headed straight down. He was barely able to pull out of his downward course in

time. God has given us his Word, our instrument panel, to guide and direct our lives. We must read it, study it, memorize it, trust it and live it.

3. *The Word of God lights the pathway of our lives.* Every member of your family must take the pathway of life, where there are dangers of sin and temptation. God's Word is the light that shines on our pathway to expose the dangers that lurk in the darkness. The psalmist declared: "Thy word is a lamp unto my feet, and a light unto my path" (Psalm 119:105, KJV).

Remember, when David wrote these words, he had a vivid understanding of the need for God's guidance and direction for his life. He had sinned and suffered miserably, because he had not leaned on God for guidance. My simple theory is this: The greater the light shines on our pathway, the clearer we can see to avoid the dangers and temptations.

Let's look at this "light on our path" concept closer. A light has no value until it is turned on. If you switch off a light, the light disappears. What changes? The light fixture is still there. The light bulb is still there. The wire, the switch, the connection are all still there. Why no light? Obviously, the switch is not turned on. The Word of God is our light. Internalizing God's Word will enlighten our minds and allow His truth to guide us through the minefield of danger and temptation. But, first we must "flip the switch" in order for its blessed light of the Word to shine.

An unknown writer has left us with the following testimony of what the Bible is to every believer:

Someone describes packing his bag for a journey. Before closing it, he observes a small corner not yet filled. He says, "Into this little corner I will put a guidebook, a lamp, a mirror, a microscope, a telescope, a volume of choice poems, several well-written biographies, a package of old letters, a book of songs, a sharp sword, and a small library of more than 60 volumes." Yet, strange enough to say, all these did not occupy a space more than three inches long by two inches wide.

"But how could you do it?"

"Well, it was all in the packing—I put in my Bible."

The Word of God is our source of strength—our survival kit for our families and one of the spiritual disciplines that can help lead us into spiritual renewal.

NOURISHING THE FAMILY

We cannot live healthy unless we nourish our bodies with food. Likewise, we cannot live in health spiritually unless we nourish our spirits with spiritual food—the living, powerful, transforming Word of God. How often do we nourish our physical bodies? I would say most of us eat quite regularly—probably several times a day. How often do we nourish our spiritual health? Regularly? Daily?

Several times a day? Think about it. Which is more important? Our physical bodies will one day perish, but our spirits will live forever.

How should we internalize the Word of God? I feel strongly that we need a daily intake of the Bible. In his book *How to Enjoy Your Bible*, John Blanchard writes:

> Surely we only have to be realistic and honest with ourselves to know how regularly we need to turn to the Bible. How often do we face problems, temptation and pressure? Every day! Then how often do we need instruction, guidance and greater encouragement? Every day! To catch all these felt needs up into an even greater issue, how often do we need to see God's face, hear his voice, feel his touch, know his power? The answer to all these questions is the same: every day! As the American evangelist D. L. Moody put it, "A man can no more take in a supply of grace for the future than he can eat enough for the next six months, or take sufficient air into his lungs at one time to sustain life for a week. We must draw upon God's boundless store of grace from day to day as we need it.[2]

Whatever our level of Bible intake, we all have the glorious opportunity to hear, read, study, memorize, meditate and experience His life-giving Word on a daily basis. Activating this spiritual discipline, along with prayer, will help ignite spiritual renewal in the home.

Memorizing the Word of God

"I have hidden your word in my heart that I might not sin against you" (Psalm 119:11).

"These commandments that I give you today are to be upon your hearts" (Deuteronomy 6:6).

Satan knows just how vitally important the Word of God is to our spiritual well-being and to our ability to impact our families spiritually. Some trivialize Scripture memorization as child's play, but I assure you, it is a serious matter to the Enemy of your soul. Satan knows that his efforts to keep you powerless and fragmented will fail if your family is daily nourished with Scriptural truths through the spiritual disciplines of Bible memorization.

Scripture memorization should be a priority in our lives. Part of Satan's deceptive plan is to make you believe your own excuses—not having a good memory, not having time, or not knowing where to start. If I were to ask you to memorize 30 verses of Scripture this month (one scripture per day), most of you would be thinking, *There is no way!* Suppose, however, I were to tell you I would give you one million dollars if you did. Would your thinking change? No amount of money I could offer you could begin to compare to the eternal value of God's Word living in your heart and mind. We're talking about real priorities. We need to live with eternal values in mind. I don't think I've ever seen a wealthy man on his deathbed ask for someone to bring his bank book, stocks, bonds or property deeds. He is more concerned about spiritual matters and family matters at that time. That's all that really matters in the end. Let's not live our lives missing the valuable treasure of the Word of God flooding our hearts and minds and leading our family to do the same.

One of the best ways to get the Word of God into your heart, and to use it effectively in your family, is to memorize it. Here are some reasons to memorize God's Word:

- Memorizing His Word gives guidance and direction to our lives. "Your statutes are my delight; they are my counselors" (Psalm 119:24).

- Memorizing His Word provides a basis for meditation. "Oh, how I love your law! I meditate on it all day long" (Psalm 119:97).

- Memorizing His Word strengthens our trust in God. "Incline your ear and hear the words of the wise, and *apply your mind* to my knowledge; for it will be pleasant if you keep them within you, that they may be ready on your lips. So that your trust may be in the Lord, I have taught you today, even you" (Proverbs 22:17-19, *NASB*).

- Memorizing His Word provides weapons to defeat Satan. "Take the helmet of salvation and the sword of the Spirit, which is the word of God" (Ephesians 6:17). In His temptation, Jesus confronted the devil, "Away from me, Satan! For it is written: 'Worship the Lord your God, and serve him only.' "(Matthew 4:10, 11). One of the most effective means to defeat Satan is to do exactly what Jesus did and say,

"It is written. . . ." That only comes from hiding the Word of God in our hearts.

Memorizing God's Word can be amazingly easy and creative. We can redeem lost time by memorizing the Word—while traveling, waiting at the doctor's office, sitting at red lights, or even rocking a baby.

Dawson Trotman, founder of the Christian organization called "The Navigators," began memorizing one Bible verse every day. He was driving a truck for a lumber yard in Los Angeles at the time. While driving around town, he would focus on his verse for that day. During the first three years of his Christian life, he memorized his first 1,000 verses. If he could memorize over 300 verses a year while driving, surely we can find ways to memorize a few.[3]

During the time I was writing this book, one of the young ladies in my Sunday school class shared a testimony about how Scripture memorization changed her father. For the last year, her dad typed Bible verses on note cards and carried them wherever he went, memorizing them. This daughter could not describe the transformation that has taken place in her dad, and the tremendous effect it has had on the rest of the family. She says he is a changed man. May I suggest that a changed man can change a family. I see it in this family.

MEDITATION ON THE WORD OF GOD

Precious promises are connected with the practice of meditation.

> Blessed is the man who does not walk in the
> counsel of the wicked or stand in the way of
> sinners or sit in the seat of mockers. But his
> delight is in the law of the Lord, and on his law
> he meditates day and night. He is like a tree
> planted by streams of water, which yields its
> fruit in season and whose leaf does not wither.
> Whatever he does prospers (Psalm 1:1-3).
>
> Do not let this Book of the Law depart from
> your mouth; meditate on it day and night, so
> that you may be careful to do everything
> written in it. Then you will be prosperous and
> successful (Joshua 1:8).

The practice of meditation is often misunder-
stood by many Christians because it has been
clouded by the rise of spiritual counterfeits and
non-Christian thinking. For this reason, many shy
away from its usage, thus allowing the Enemy to
rob them of a tremendous tool for internalizing the
Word of God. The term *meditation* is often associat-
ed today with yoga, transcendental meditation,
relaxation therapy or even the New Age movement. But in its original concept, meditation was
given by God for His people. We must not allow
Satan to steal this precious gift from our families.

Meditation helps Christians go beyond hearing,
studying and even memorization. It is a spiritual
means of absorbing God's Word. Donald S. Whitney
explains how Biblical meditation works. In his book
Spiritual Disciplines for the Christian Life, meditation is
defined as deep thinking on the truths and spiritual

realities revealed in Scripture for the purposes of understanding, application and prayer.

> You are a cup of hot water and the intake of Scripture is represented by the tea bag. Hearing God's Word is like one dip of the tea bag into the cup. Some of the tea's flavor is absorbed by the water, but not as much as would occur with a more thorough soaking of the bag. In this analogy, reading, studying and memorizing God's Word are represented by additional plunges of the tea bag into the cup. The more frequently the tea enters the water, the more effect it has. Meditation, however, is like immersing the bag completely and letting it steep until all the rich tea flavor has been extracted and the hot water is thoroughly tinctured reddish-brown.[4]

It is obvious that this kind of spiritual meditation on God's Word differs from the counterfeit groups. Christian meditation does not advocate relaxing in order to empty your mind—it encourages you to fill your mind with the thoughts of God and His life-changing truths. "Finally, brothers, whatever is true, whatever is noble, whatever is right, whatever is pure, whatever is lovely, whatever is admirable—if anything is excellent or praiseworthy—think about such things" (Philippians 4:8). What we choose to put in our minds determines what comes out in our words and actions.

A very important aspect of meditation is prayer. Too often we read the Bible, close it quickly and start praying. Meditation can be an exciting link between Bible study and prayer. This scripture shows the connection: "May the words of my mouth and the meditation of my heart be pleasing in your sight, O Lord, my Rock and my Redeemer" (Psalm 19:14).

Here's how it works: First, we read the Word of God. Then we spend time meditating, soaking in His Word, digesting it and memorizing it. Then we talk to God and ask Him to enlighten, inspire, and instruct us.

George Mueller made a life-changing discovery about the connection between meditation and prayer in his own life. It literally transformed his spiritual life. Does this sound like what you want for you and your family? He described his new insight this way:

> Before this time my practice has been, at least for ten years previously, as an habitual thing, to give myself to prayer after having dressed in the morning. Now, I saw that the most important thing was to give myself to the reading of God's Word, and to meditation on it, that thus my heart might be comforted, encouraged, warned, reproved, instructed; and that thus, by means of the Word of God, whilst meditating on it, my heart might be brought into experimental communion with the Lord.
>
> I began therefore to meditate on the New Testament from the beginning, early in the morning. The first thing I did, after having

asked a few words of the Lord's blessing upon
His precious Word, was to begin to meditate
on the Word of God, searching as it were into
every verse to get blessing out of it; not for the
sake of the public ministry of the Word, not
for the sake of preaching on what I had medi-
tated upon, but for the sake of obtaining food
for my own soul.[5]

Thomas Manton, noted Puritan preacher and
writer, writes about the link between meditation on
the Word and prayer:

Meditation is a middle sort of duty between
the Word and prayer, and hath respect to
both. The Word feedeth meditation, and
meditation feedeth prayer. These duties must
always go hand in hand; meditation must follow hearing and precede prayer.[6]

An old maxim sums it up: "Memorizing puts the
Word of God in your head, but meditating puts the
Word of God in your heart."[7]

Experiencing Biblical Truth

The Word of God is our source of spiritual
nourishment and strength. It is the family's weapon
of warfare and God's written revelation to us.
However, the key to activating these blessings in our
lives is to experience God personally — to obey Him
and apply His Word to our lives on a daily basis.

There is a story of a soap manufacturer and a pastor who were walking down a street in a large city. The soap manufacturer casually said, "The gospel you preach hasn't done much good, has it? Just observe. There is still a lot of wickedness in the world, and a lot of wicked people, too!" The pastor made no reply until they passed a dirty little child making mud pies in the gutter. Seizing the opportunity, the pastor said, "I see that the soap you make hasn't done much good in the world. There is much dirt, and many dirty people around." The soap manufacturer replied, "Oh, well, soap is only useful when it is applied." And the pastor said, "Exactly, so it is with the gospel."[8] We can build a spiritual home by leading our families to "experience" the following scriptures:

> These commandments that I give you today are to be upon your hearts. *Impress* them on your children. Talk about them when you sit at home and when you walk along the road, when you lie down and when you get up (Deuteronomy 6:6, 7).

There is blessing promised for families who obey the Word of God. "Now that you know these things, you will be blessed if you do them" (John 13:17). "Do not merely listen to the word, and so deceive yourselves. Do what it says" (James 1:22).

It is possible for us to hear the Word of God, study it, pray about it, meditate upon it and even memorize it, but still not obey it and experience it.

We will not see the fruit of it in our lives and in our
family if we don't *live* it.

Jesus contrasts the folly of not obeying His
words with the wisdom of living them out in
everyday life:

> "Why do you call me, 'Lord, Lord,' and do not
> do what I say? I will show you what he is like
> who comes to me and hears my words and
> puts them into practice. He is like a man build-
> ing a house, who dug down deep and laid the
> foundation on rock. When a flood came, the
> torrent struck that house but could not shake
> it, because it was well built. But the one who
> hears my words and does not put them into
> practice is like a man who built a house on the
> ground without a foundation. The moment
> the torrent struck that house, it collapsed and
> its destruction was complete" (Luke 6:46-49).

Notice the difference in the two men and these
two houses. Both heard, but only one responded;
therefore, only this man's house was able to stand.
Think about your own spiritual home. It, too, must
be built on a solid rock foundation of obedience to
God's Word. This necessitates experiencing the
Word of God in our families. "Therefore everyone
who hears these words of mine and puts them into
practice is like a wise man who built his house on
the rock" (Matthew 7:24).

Unless Biblical truth takes the 18-inch plunge
from our head to our hearts and then another
plunge to our hands and feet, it will never change

our lives. That's why a critical part of our family life is the need to experience Biblical truth.[9]

Experiencing the Bible simply means "living out" the Word of God in our lives. We must go beyond leading our families in learning the Word of God and obeying it; we must challenge them to experience what they have learned. Reading, hearing and even seeing is important, but saying and doing (experiencing God's Word) takes our walk with God to a new level.

In my teaching at Lee University and conducting teacher training conferences, I strongly encourage teachers to involve their students. Students should be "active participators and not passive spectators." The following statistics support the importance participation plays in the learning process. Most people remember:

- Only 10 percent of what they read.

- Only 20 percent of what they hear.

- Only 30 percent of what they see.

- About 50 percent of what they see and hear together.

- About 70 percent of what they say.

- About 90 percent of what they do (active participation).[10]

It is easy to see that the more we experience the Word, the more likely it becomes a permanent part of the fabric of our heart, mind and soul.

Here are a few ideas of how we can personally experience Bible verses:

- "It is more blessed to give than to receive" (Acts 20:35). Give your spouse and family members a hug each morning. Give a few minutes to help each family member with a chore. Share a prayer of blessing with family members before bedtime each night. This kind of giving requires thinking less of yourself and thinking more of ways to bless your family. When practicing this Bible verse, you will feel the power of its truth.

- "Therefore encourage one another and build each other up, just as in fact you are doing" (1 Thessalonians 5:11). Encourage different members of your family by telling them how much you appreciate them. Tell them you will be praying for them, and pray for them right there on the spot.

- "Rejoice with those who rejoice, and weep with those who weep" (Romans 12:15, *NKJV*). When family members meet goals or accomplish special feats, rejoice with them. At the same time, be ready to weep with a family member who experiences a sadness, hurt or pain. Express encouragement and empathy by saying, "It hurts me to see you hurt." Refrain from "It'll be OK," or "Don't worry about it, everything will be fine," or "It's not that big of a deal."

- "Do not let any unwholesome talk come out of your mouths, but only what is helpful for building others up according to their needs, that it may benefit those who listen" (Ephesians 4:29). Share uplifting scriptures with your family each day. When you speak a harsh or hurtful word, apologize immediately and ask that family member to pray with you for strength to speak only wholesome words.

Hearing, reading, studying, memorizing, meditating, obeying and experiencing the Word of God are building blocks for spiritual renewal.
The Lord declares:

As the rain and the snow come down from heaven, and do not return to it without watering the earth and making it bud and flourish, so that it yields seed for the sower and bread for the eater, so is my word that goes out from my mouth: It will not return to me empty, but will accomplish what I desire and achieve the purpose for which I sent it (Isaiah 55:10, 11).

5
Nurturing a Servant's Heart in Your Family

Unamuno, the Spanish philosopher, tells about the Roman aqueduct at Segovia, in his native Spain. It was built in A.D. 109. For 1800 years, it carried cool water from the mountains to the hot and thirsty city. Nearly 60 generations of men drank from its flow. Then came another generation, a recent one, who said, "This aqueduct is so great a marvel that it ought to be preserved for our children, as a museum piece. We shall relieve it of its centuries-long labor." They laid modern iron pipes and gave the ancient bricks and mortar a reverent rest. And the aqueduct began to fall apart. The sun beating on the dry mortar caused it to crumble. The bricks and stone sagged and threatened to fall. What ages of service could not destroy idleness disintegrated.[1]

A related story is told of the great violinist, Nicolo Paganini, who willed his marvelous violin to Genoa — the city of his birth — but only on condition that the instrument never be played upon. It

was an unfortunate condition, for it is a peculiarity
of wood that as long as it is used and handled, it
shows little wear. As soon as it is discarded, it
begins to decay. The exquisite, mellow-toned violin
has become worm-eaten in its beautiful case, val-
ueless except as a relic. The moldering instrument
is a reminder that a life withdrawn from all service
to others loses its meaning.[2]

Looking for ways to bless others shows the true
spirit of servanthood. We all want our families to
exemplify a spirit of Christlikeness. That can only
be evidenced by a lifestyle of unselfish service. In
the Gospel of Mark, Jesus is portrayed as Servant.
A servant's heart is consumed with giving and
serving others. This lifestyle of serving will be
infectious in our families and will help ignite a
renewal of Christlikeness in our lives.

Nurturing a Giving Spirit

Love manifests itself — you can't hide it! James
states in his writings that if you have faith, you
will also have works. "Faith without works is
dead" (James 2:26, KJV). The same is true with
love. Love that doesn't give, serve, or show kindness is not love. Our actions speak louder than
our words.

We are known by our fruit. We can scream to the
top of our lungs that we are an apple tree, but if we
have oranges growing on our limbs, we are not an
apple tree. We can talk the talk, but our family is
watching our walk.

An old saying addresses the relationship between giving and loving: "You can give without loving, but you can't love without giving." An insightful true story illustrates this spirit of giving:

> A monk who was traveling in the mountains found a precious stone in a stream. The next day he met another traveler who was hungry, and the monk opened his bag to share his food. The hungry traveler saw the precious stone in the monk's bag, admired it, and asked the monk to give it to him. The monk did so without hesitation.
>
> The traveler left, rejoicing in his good fortune. He knew the jewel was worth enough to give him security for the rest of his life.
>
> But a few days later he came back searching for the monk. When he found him, he returned the stone and said, "I have been thinking. I know how valuable this stone is, but I give it back to you in the hope that you can give me something much more precious. If you can, give me what you have within you that enabled you to give me the stone."[3]

The monk possessed something far more precious than a priceless jewel—a giving spirit. Psalm 112:5 tells us, "Good will come to him who is generous and lends freely." God wants us to be generous people—generous in giving of ourselves to our spouses and our children. Charles Swindoll gets to the heart of the matter when he said, "We are never more like God than when we give."[4]

An old sermon illustration communicates the dynamic results of giving. There are two seas in the land of Palestine—the Dead Sea and the Sea of Galilee. The Dead Sea is putrid and stale. It has no vegetation or life in it. A few miles away, the Sea of Galilee is a fresh and clean body of water, teeming with life. The difference is simple. The Dead Sea receives and *keeps*, while the Sea of Galilee receives and *gives*.

Jesus' life epitomized giving. God *gave* Jesus, His only begotten Son. And Jesus *gave* His life, so that we can live victoriously and have eternal life. It was the supreme gift. Therefore Christians must have a giving spirit if we are to be like Him and reflect His character. This involves more that giving in tithes and offerings. It means giving our best time, love, words of affirmation, understanding, respect and appreciation. That is how we reflect God in our daily lifestyle.

Sacrificial Giving

Jesus said: "Give, and it will be given to you. A good measure, pressed down, shaken together and running over, will be poured into your lap. For with the measure you use, it will be measured to you" (Luke 6:38). This law of giving applies to several areas of our lives, but it especially applies to family relationships. Remember, marriage and family were the first relationships God created. That places a high priority on them. Giving of our time *and* ourselves reaps rich benefits — deeper and stronger family relationships.

Sacrificial giving involves husband/wife relationships and parent/child relationship. This principle is clearly communicated in Philippians 2:3: "Do nothing out of selfish ambition or vain conceit, but in humility consider others better than yourselves." Sacrificial giving doesn't just say "I love you." It shows "I love you" by focusing on other family members' needs. This happens naturally when we heed the words of Jesus: "A new command I give you: Love one another. As I have loved you, so you must love one another" (John 13:34). This is the essence of giving — putting others first!

Ron Hutchcraft writes in *Start Your Trip With a Full Tank*:

> Something's missing in so many marriages today, isn't it? Instead of creating a glow, it's creating stress. What's missing? Perhaps the missing ingredient is three little words that the minister who married us shared as we left on our honeymoon. He said, "I didn't have time to do marriage counseling. I'm sorry, but I'll give you the three words the minister gave to me on our wedding night. They'll last you the rest of your marriage: Put her first." Or put him first. Now, that doesn't resolve all of the issues, but it sure is a great place to start. I think those are words that most relationships start with but lose when selfishness takes over. Put him first. Put her first. It sounds risky, but that's the nature of love.[5]

When members of the family become consumed
with meeting the needs of other family members,
an explosion of love takes place. Since God is love,
He will permeate every facet of our family.

Sacrificial giving is not conditional—we don't
give in order to receive. We must follow the admonition of Acts 20:35: "It is more blessed to give than
to receive." Unconditional love does not say:

- I'll love you and give to you if . . .

- I'll love you and give to you because . . .

- I'll love you and give to you when . . .

These conditions destroy healthy family relationships. The body of Christ is instructed to be giving
to "one another." The *Intimate Life Ministries
Handbook* outlines this aspect of God's plan for His
people. These admonitions are mentioned numer-
ous times in the Bible:

"Greet one another" — 26 times

"Comfort one another" — 6 times

"Love one another" — 16 times

"Teach one another" — 4 times

"Admonish one another" — 2 times

"Honor one another" — 2 times

"Be devoted to one another" — 1 time

"Bear one another's burdens" — 2 times

"Accept one another" — 1 time

"Forgive one another" — 3 times

"Serve one another" — 4 times[6]

God is pleased when He sees His children comforting one another, loving one another, forgiving one another, honoring one another and serving one another! That's what happens in a relationship that characterizes "mutual" giving.

UNSELFISHNESS

The Bible tells us, "Do nothing out of selfish ambition or vain conceit, but in humility consider others better than yourselves" (Philippians 2:3).

Selfishness is easy and natural. It seeks its own . . . demands . . . takes . . . manipulates . . . destroys marital and family relationships. Many couples I have counseled with want me to straighten out their spouse. It goes something like this: "There she is, Dr. Seals, tell her what her role is in this marriage. It is to submit. That's what the Bible says, doesn't it? Go ahead and tell her!" What is interesting to me is that some of these husbands do not even know John 3:16, but they can quote "Wives, submit" every time.

Selfishness is a preoccupation with self. It means "my way at everybody else's expense." But Jesus, our role model, demands the opposite.

A scenario of selfishness plays out in real life something like this:

A husband who is ready for church waits in the car for his family. His wife is late. He keeps waiting. She doesn't come out to the car. He toots the horn. Still no wife or kids. In anger, he lays down on the horn, sending the message to the family inside: "Hurry and get out here . . . I'm tired of waiting for you!"

Not a pretty picture of Christlikeness, but a scene that will be played out in a driveway near you this weekend. It would have been better for the husband to help his family get ready before he ever got in the car. This requires thinking of others more than yourself. I read about a lady who told her husband that they were going to change roles for the day. She said that he could get all of the children dressed while she went outside and blew the car horn.

An example of true unselfishness is depicted in this story:

> Sidney would come home from work drained. But three hungry children had to be fed. Over the years he had become fairly efficient. Little, eager hands would do a childish job of setting the table while his tired hands worked over the stove. Laughs and lectures would make the dinner ritual more than substance for the body—it was also an investment in a lifetime.
>
> Dishes would be washed, clean pajamas would replace the clothes that bore the marks of a day of adventures, and stories and prayers would help sleepy eyes drift from the cares of the day to the quiet and safety of slumber.

That's when Sidney would retire to the back corner of the house. He'd say goodbye to the day nurse and then complete the rest of his evening ritual. A catheter bag had to be emptied and a bed pan had to be offered. He would take a clean wash cloth and warm water to wash the face of his bride. It had been a couple of years since the accident. Yet his vows were clear: "For better or for worse." It could have been him who had been hit by the drunk. Instead, it was the woman he loved.

He would tell her all the good things about his day, never the worries. He knew that she loved music, so he'd hum her a few tunes from their past. Then he'd look into her eyes and tell her what he told her every night before she went to sleep and every morning when she woke up. "I love you, honey. You're my life, my love, and my wife."[7]

A sobering question we must ask ourselves is, Are we a "taker" or are we a "giver"? Our walk with God determines the answer. It also determines the spiritual impact we have in our home.

ACTS OF SERVICE

Matthew 20:28 portrays the life of Christ like this: "The Son of Man did not come to be served, but to serve, and to give his life as a ransom for many." The apostle Paul sets the example:

Your attitude should be the same as that of
Christ Jesus: Who, being in very nature God,
did not consider equality with God something to be grasped, but made himself nothing, taking the very nature of a servant, being
made in human likeness. And being found in
appearance as a man, he humbled himself
and became obedient to death—even death
on a cross! (Philippians 2:5-8).

A special blessing is given to servants of God in
John 12:26: "Whoever serves me must follow me;
and where I am, my servant also will be. My Father
will honor the one who serves me."

What a blessing! We can enjoy rich fellowship
with Jesus when we serve. We will also be honored
by God the Father. Intimate family relationships
grow in an environment of serving one another. Jill
Briscoe shares this story about service in her family:

Stuart talked about the family we might have,
and we let our minds race ahead to the incredible blessing and miracle of little eternal people in the shape of boys or girls. "I'd want our
kids to be part of it all," Stuart said.

"Oh yes," I echoed excitedly. "The text says,
'As for me and my house, we will serve the
Lord.' I don't want to watch you doing it, with-
out doing it myself," I told my fiancé. "And
I'm sure you don't want to watch me doing
my thing while you twiddle your thumbs.
What's more, I'm doubly convinced we don't

want our kids standing passively on the side-
lines cheering us both on." We agreed we
wanted the whole family caught up in the glorious possibilities of serving Christ together.[8]

There are two things Christian families need
to do to obey the commands of Christ to be "others" oriented.

1. *Parents model acts of service.* It may mean helping someone with a flat tire, running errands for
the elderly, watering plants for neighbors who are
on vacation, taking food to a needy family at
Thanksgiving or Christmas, working at a fund-
raising event for the handicapped or carrying a tray
for an elderly person at a restaurant. Or it may
mean taking your spouse a cup of coffee when you
make yourself one, serving your child breakfast in
bed or doing a family member's chores for them. I
know one husband who warms up his wife and
daughter's cars on cold mornings so that they can
have a nice warm car to drive to work and school.
Another husband prepares a big breakfast for the
entire family on Saturday mornings so his wife can
sleep. Whatever the situation, children need to see
parents living a lifestyle of service.

2. *Involve your children in acts of service.* Let them
help you discuss, plan and perform a significant act
of service each month. This attitude of service con-
tributes significantly to the spiritual health of our
families. Acts of kindness within the family helps
develop a mind-set for service.

Albert Einstein displayed the portraits of two
scientists—Newton and Maxwell—on his walls.

Toward the end of his life, he replaced those two with the portraits of Gandhi and Schwertzer. Einstein explained that it was time to replace the image of *success* with the image of *service*.[9]

If you study the history of men and women who were dedicated to sacrificial giving, you will find that most came from homes where service was a very important part of their value system.

Service Motivated by Love

We cannot hide our motives from God, and usually our family can see through insincerity. Our service should not come only in times of conven- ience, or when it will benefit ourselves. Whether ministering at church or helping with the children at home, service requires the right motive.

Richard Foster addresses the issue of motive very well:

> Self-righteous service requires external re- wards. It needs to know that people see and appreciate the effort. It seeks human applause—with proper religious modesty of course. . . . Self-righteous service is highly concerned about results. It eagerly wants to see if the person served will reciprocate in kind. . . . The flesh whines against service but screams against hidden service. It strains and pulls for honor and recognition. It will devise subtle, religiously acceptable means to call attention to the service rendered.[10]

Proper motives will be guided by love and obedience. Our motives should serve Christ. In taking the title "Christian," we agree to be like Him, to have His heart.

We should also be motivated by forgiveness. Read the words of Donald S. Whitney:

> The people of God do not serve Him in order to be forgiven but because we are forgiven. When believers serve only because they feel guilty if they don't, it's as though they serve with a ball and chain dragging from their ankles. There's no love in that kind of service, only labor. There's no joy, only obligation and drudgery. But Christians aren't prisoners who should serve in God's Kingdom grudgingly because of guilt. We can serve willingly because Christ's death freed us from guilt.[11]

We don't serve others to receive recognition from them or to score points with God. We don't serve others to make us feel good, even though that may be a by-product. We don't serve our spouses or our children so that they will love and appreciate us more. We don't serve them to get them to love us more. We serve because we love.

Gary Chapman, in his book *Five Signs of a Functional Family*, comes to this conclusion:

> "It is a great paradox that the way up is down. True greatness is expressed in serving, not in dominating. No parents challenge their children to be like Hitler, while thousands

continue to challenge their children to be like Jesus. Service is a mark of greatness."[12]

Part III

LIVING IN THE HOUSE OF SPIRITUAL RENEWAL

Once the spiritual foundation is laid and the home is built with the essential spiritual building materials, families can begin to experience a renewal in their relationships. Spiritual renewal dramatically affects the way we live, love, forgive, speak, spend our time, and eventually the legacy we leave.

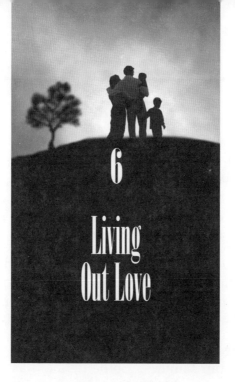

6

Living Out Love

Love is the cement that holds families together. For spiritual renewal to occur in your family, this love has to be actualized. The popular song "Love Is a Verb," sung by DC Talk, basically says that love is a matter of action, not a matter of words.

Many parents feel they are short on the love required to raise a godly family. These parents usually come from families that did not know how to show their love to each other. Therefore, they must learn new ways of loving their families.

In today's society, many people describe love as an abstract feeling that comes and goes with the experiences of life. God wants families to know the power of love and to experience its lasting impact. Spiritual renewal involves an awakening to the kind of love that God has for His families.

LOVE DEFINED

The Biblical understanding of love must be revisited. The following are three Greek words for love:

- *Eros* is sexual or physical intimacy. The New Testament does not use this word.

- *Phileo* connotes companionship or friendship. Philadelphia, "the city of brotherly love," was named after this word. Phileo characterizes the relationship between best friends.

- *Agape* is the kind of love desperately needed in our families. Some define it as unconditional positive regard. It is the love-in-action, no-strings-attached kind of love that God has for us. It is the word used in Ephesians 5:25: "Husbands, love your wives, just as Christ loved the church and gave himself up for her." This is the love that God wants parents to learn and model to each other and to their children.

These three types of love should be in every family, but the underlying current that powers it comes from God the Father. His love working through us enables families to "live out" love.[1] This kind of love is where the following emotional needs are met:

- Affection (1 Thessalonians 2:8)

- Appreciation (1 Corinthians 11:2)

- Approval (Romans 14:18)

- Attention (1 Corinthians 12:25)

- Acceptance (Romans 15:7)

- Comfort (2 Corinthians 1:3-4)

- Encouragement (1 Thessalonians 5:11)

- Respect (1 Peter 2:17)

- Security (1 John 4:18)

- Support (Galatians 6:2)[2]

Jesus said that the wise man builds his house upon the rock (Matthew 7:24). A house that is built on the solid rock of unconditional love will stand the storms of life. The following illustration further explains the importance of *agape* love and how it helps couples stand:

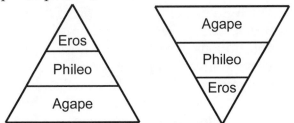

The first triangle depicts the house built upon *agape* love. When the foundation is built on the love of God, no storm can bring it down. Other kinds of love are included in this house, but they are not the foundation. The Egyptian pyramids are an example to this concept.

The second triangle shows how easy it is for a marriage to fail when the foundation is built on feeling (*eros* love) alone. The triangle is easily toppled by a small windstorm. Couples who monitor their relationship by the feeling of love will not last. They must be grounded in the love of God.

Children who are not loved unconditionally battle insecurity. They are easy targets of rejection, ridicule, and other hurts. On the other hand, when children are given unconditional love at home, they are much stronger against these hurts.[3]

Living Out Unconditional Love

For most contemporary families, unconditional love has to be learned. Love is a choice, based on 1 Corinthians 13 as a blueprint.

Love is patient. When couples first marry, they have inflated perceptions of their roles. They soon discover that their relationship has changed somewhat. The feelings of love may begin to fade. Little things start to irritate. These are prime opportunities for demonstrations of patience and learning ways to share without anger. Patience permits growth and allows for mistakes. Joseph Parker tells a story of how a wife's patience with her unsaved husband eventually resulted in his conversion. At first, she was very impatient with him. She shared this with her pastor, and he encouraged her to keep living her Christian life at home. A few days later her husband came in after a hunting trip and accidentally broke her favorite lamp. He knew he deserved a fiery verbal attack from his wife. His wife came in and patiently and lovingly told him it was all right, and gave him a hug and kiss. Within a week, the man, softened by love, was converted.[4]

The same principles can be applied to your children. Children deserve patience. You do not expect them to grasp everything you teach them. Listen patiently to them. Appropriate family models of love will take time to build.

Love is kind. One of the manifestations of the fruit of the Spirit is kindness. A sign of being spiritually renewed is practicing kindness. One of the greatest examples of kindness is the story of Ruth and Boaz (Ruth 2:11). Boaz was kind by leaving extra grain in the field so that Ruth would have more for her family (3:15-17).

A husband can show kindness to his wife by offering to cook or doing out-of-the-ordinary chores for his wife. A wife can prepare her husband his favorite meal, even if she does not like that particular food.

Love is never jealous or envious. Christian relationships must be built on trust. Henry Overstreet states:

> The love of a person implies, not the possession of that person, but the affirmation of that person. It means granting him, gladly, the full right of his/her humanhood. One does not truly love a person and yet seek to enslave him by law or by bonds of dependence and possessiveness.[5]

True love allows freedom for other friendships and pursuits.

Love is never boastful or proud. Pride keeps us from admitting our mistakes. It keeps us living in our own world—the loneliest place to live. Pride says: "I am the only person who has needs."

Love is never haughty or selfish. A marriage is not a 50/50 relationship. It is a 100/100 relationship, each concerned with the other's needs.

Love is not rude. After a while, couples may begin to take each other for granted. They demand. They do not say "please" or "thank you." Respect is a basic requirement for emotional maturity. Couples must maintain respect for each other by being thoughtful.

Love does not demand its own way. Love never manipulates or ridicules anyone to have emotional needs met. Expressing your needs to your spouse without making your spouse feel defensive is important. One way to do this is to use "I" messages versus "you" messages. For example, saying "I feel lonely when you are gone," rather than, "You're never around!"

Love is not irritable or touchy. Being irritable or touchy often is the result of not knowing how to handle criticism or conflict. We must learn to separate criticisms and disagreements without devaluing each other. Adult children of divorced parents often have this problem. They have watched their parents argue and vowed they would never do the same. Consequently, they fail to develop effective methods handling anger. True love will overlook petty differences.

Love does not hold grudges. Love demands that couples learn to forgive, and not "keep a record of wrongs." Forgiveness does not mean that we forget—forgetting is much harder. Forgiveness means allowing each other time and space to work through hurtful situations.

Love rejoices over the truth. Often when couples face

trials or major decisions, power struggles ensue. The husband is the head of the family, but his headship is won by sacrificial giving to his wife. A wife usually finds it easier to happily submit to this type of leadership. Nevertheless, there are times when a solution to a problem is not clear to either spouse. As couples jostle for power, wounds are inflicted, often fatally. As couples we should then prayerfully seek for truth and peace in difficult situations.

Love goes on forever. The love God builds in your home has a manufacturer's warranty that lasts forever. Children who grow up in these types of homes enjoy the same guarantee. Human ways of showing God's love are passed from generation to generation, warming the hearts and lighting the homes of your children's children.[6]

DISCOVERING YOUR CHILD'S LOVE LANGUAGE

The primary need of a child is to feel loved. This is accomplished by learning their language of love.

Everyone experiences love differently. The following are the five languages of love outlined by Gary Chapman in his book *Five Signs of a Functional Family*:

- Words of affirmation
- Quality time
- Physical touch
- Receiving gifts
- Acts of service[7]

To discover your child's love language, you must first observe the way the child expresses love to you. If your son consistently says you are a good parent, then his language may be words of affirmation. Second, listen to what your children ask of you most often. If your child consistently asks you to bring back a gift from a trip, then this child's primary love language is receiving gifts. Asking, "How did I do?" indicates a need for words of affirmation. Finally, listen to what your children complain about most often. If you hear criticism because you never play with them, then they need quality time.

If you are still trying to discover your child's love language, focus on a different language each month and observe how your child responds. When you are speaking their language, they will be much more responsive to your teaching and training. They will tend to be more positive, because they feel secure.

PURSUING INTIMACY

At first glance, this heading may conjure up wild notions of the physical aspect of love. That's OK. That part of loving your mate is very important too. God intended sex to be a wonderful and enriching part of the marriage relationship.

Marital intimacy is not something that you schedule or decree. It can't be taken off the shelf and put back like a book. Neither can it be demanded. It must develop during the day-to-day and week-to-week process of relating to each other as husband and wife, friends, spiritual encouragers and lovers.

I have heard intimacy defined as "in-to-me-see" —

look inside me and see me as a person. What are my values? What are my opinions? What is my favorite color? How do I feel about certain issues? What makes me tick? Real intimacy produces closeness and kinship.

But what are some practical suggestions for pursuing intimacy?

1. *Say love.* Start by simply saying, "I love you." I realize that talk can be cheap, but you still need to affirm your mate. When a wife asks her husband, "Did you enjoy that nice meal I prepared for you?" The inappropriate response is, "I'm eating it, ain't I?" When a wife asks her husband, "Sweetheart, do you still love me?" the inappropriate response is, "I told you when we got married, and I'll let you know if I change my mind." Not good! Love needs to be spoken. Our mates need to hear words of love, companionship and devotion. Here are a few practical suggestions:

- Compliment your mate at least once every day.

- Talk about your future.

- Call your spouse during the day.

- Apologize if you hurt your mate's feelings.

- Ask what you can do to make his/her day more enjoyable.

- Pray out loud for or with your spouse.

- Say, "I love you," regularly.

2. *Do* love. The list above will reinforce your love, but don't stop there. Do something! Show your love in tangible ways. Here are a few ideas:

- Smile at your mate often.

- Give gifts . . . the more personal the better.

- Hold hands often.

- Try to always look your best for your mate.

- Always wear your wedding ring and flash it often.

- Be polite, gentle and kind.

- Start every day with a hug and a kiss.

- End every day with a hug and a kiss.

3. *Write* love. A very special way to communicate love and develop intimacy is to express your love in writing. My wife has saved every letter I have written to her. I'm not talking about the love notes when we were dating, but the ones I write to her now, after 25 years of marriage. Letters written for no particular occasion work best.

One particularly thoughtful note was shared by Paul Harvey:

> Carl Coleman was driving to work when he bumped fenders with another motorist. Both cars stopped, and the woman driving the other car got out to survey the damage. She was distraught. It was her fault, she admitted, and

hers was a new car, less than two days from the showroom. She dreaded facing her husband. Coleman was sympathetic; but he had to pursue the exchange of license and registration data. She reached into her glove compartment to retrieve the documents in an envelope. On the first paper to tumble out, written in her husband's distinctive hand, were these words: "In case of an accident, remember, Honey, it's you I love, not the car."[8]

Here are a few other ways to express your love in writing:

- Send cards in season and out of season.

- Place "I love you" notes in obvious locations for your spouse to find.

- Write a poem. (Husbands, this will show love and provide some laughter.)

4. *Keep love.* Focusing on romance is not unspiritual. As a matter of fact, it is Biblical. The Bible is a romantic book. The Books of Ruth, Esther and the Song of Solomon offer a few suggestions to help husbands and wives fan the flames of love. Partners must never take each other or their marriage for granted. This is depicted quite well by Art Sueltz, who satirized the stages of the common cold in seven years of marriage:

First year: "Sugar, I'm worried about my little baby girl. You've got a bad sniffle. I want to put you in the hospital for a complete check-up. I know the food is lousy, so I've arranged for your meals to be sent up from Rossini's."

Second year: "Listen, honey, I don't like the sound of that cough. I've called Dr. Miller and he's going to rush right over. Now will you go to bed like a good girl just for me, please?"

Third year: "Maybe you'd better lie down, honey. Nothing like a little rest if you're feeling bad. I'll bring you something to eat. Have we got any soup in the house?"

Fourth year: "Look, dear. Be sensible. After you've fed the kids and washed the dishes, you'd better hit the sack."

Fifth year: "Why don't you take a couple of aspirin?"

Sixth year: "If you'd just gargle or something instead of sitting around barking like a seal."

Seventh year: "For heaven's sake, stop sneezing. What are you trying to do, give me pneumonia?"[9]

It shouldn't be that way, and it doesn't have to be that way. Love is a verb, a choice, and so is our commitment. Here are a few suggestions to help keep love alive:

- Cuddle often.

- Wink at each other — one eye first, then the other, then both (my daughter taught me this one.)

- Plan a date each week — put it in your planners.

- Touch often.

- Send flowers just to say "I love you."

- Plan a romantic getaway once or twice a year.

5. *Listen for love.* Adrian Rodgers shares a story about an old couple who were sitting by the fireside. He looked over at her, had a romantic thought, and said, "After 50 years, I've found you tried and true." The wife's hearing wasn't very good, so she said, "What?" He repeated, "After 50 years, I've found you tried and true." She replied, "After 50 years, I'm tired of you, too."[10] Something was lost in that communication process. The Bible has a lot to say about the way we communicate with each other. God made us with two ears, but only one mouth. That ought to give us a hint about His view of the communication process. Paul warns us in Ephesians 4:29 to say "only what is helpful for building others up according to their needs." James tells us that "everyone should be quick to listen, slow to speak and slow to become angry" (1:19).

Listening is not only the key to effective communication, it is also a key to a loving marital relationship. A teacher once asked his students what was the difference between listening and hearing. After a long pause, one pupil finally replied, "Listening is wanting to hear." The message that needs to be sent is, "I love you enough to listen." Here are a few practical guidelines to hear love:

- Listen with your heart. Listen for feelings, not just words.

- Listen with your eyes. Look at your mate when he/she is communicating, and stay focused.

- Don't be thinking about other things.

- Don't interrupt.

- Be slow to speak, slow to anger, and quick to listen.

6. *Live love.* The Bible gives us a vivid portrait of God's love for us: "How great is the love the Father has lavished on us, that we should be called children of God!" (1 John 3:1).

This scripture provides a wonderful pattern of how to function in our families. Just as God, our Father, lavishes love on us, so should we lavish love on our mate and children. Spiritual renewal flourishes in an atmosphere of love lived and expressed.

Living out love involves making a commitment. It involves sacrifice and demands our best. Renewal in your home requires that each of us *say* love, *do* love, *write* love, *keep* love, *hear* love, and *live* love. The words of Frank Outlaw show how our love grows:

Watch your thoughts; they become words,
Watch your words; they become actions,
Watch your actions; they become habits,
Watch your habits; they become character,
Watch your character; it becomes your destiny.[11]

7

Practicing Forgiveness

In 1971, a group of Japanese pastors traveling through Korea, came upon a memorial. Many years earlier the monument had been built by Koreans at the site where the Japanese burned a church filled with Korean families. They doused it with kerosene, and burned it to the ground, as an armed group of Japanese stood outside to prevent anyone from escaping. The Korean families knew it was the end. As they sang and the children wailed, all was lost in the deafening roar of the flames. The bitterness of this cruelty had been passed down to a new generation. The monument was now a symbol that memorialized all the people who suffered and perished. Here's how Tim Kimmel tells the rest of the story:

> When the group of Japanese pastors read the details of the tragedy and the names of the spiritual brothers and sisters who perished, they were overcome with shame.

Their country had sinned, and even though none of them were personally involved (some were not even born at the time of the tragedy), they still felt a national guilt that could not be excused.

They returned to Japan committed to right a wrong. There was an immediate outpouring of love from their fellow believers. They raised ten million yen ($25,000). The money was transferred through proper channels and a beautiful white church building was erected on the sight of the tragedy.

When the dedication service for the new building was held, a delegation from Japan joined the relatives and special guests. Although their generosity was acknowledged and their attempts at making peace appreciated, the memories were still there.

Hatred preserves pain. It keeps the wounds open and the hurts fresh. The Koreans' bitterness had festered for decades. Christian brothers or not, these Japanese were descendants of a ruthless enemy.

As the song leader closed the service with the hymn "At the Cross," the normally stoic Japanese could not contain themselves. The tears that began to fill their eyes during the song suddenly gushed from deep inside. They

turned to their Korean spiritual relatives and
begged them to forgive.

The guarded, calloused hearts of the Koreans
were not quick to surrender. But the love
of the Japanese believers — unintimidated
by decades of hatred — tore at the Koreans'
emotions.

At the cross, at the cross
Where I first saw the light,
And the burden of my heart rolled away . . .

One Korean turned toward a Japanese brother. Then another. And then the floodgates
holding back a wave of emotion let go. The
Koreans met their new Japanese friends in the
middle. They clung to each other and wept.
Japanese tears of repentance and Korean tears
of forgiveness intermingled to bathe the site
of an old nightmare.

Heaven had sent the gift of reconciliation to a
little white church in Korea.[1]

The need for forgiveness in marriage and family
relationships may not be as major in scope as the
Korean-Japanese ordeal, but it is just as important.

God Forgives and He Wants Us to Forgive

To understand and practice forgiveness is what
God desires for families. Forgiveness should be

a way of life in our homes. It is the very heart of God. God gave His Son so that He could forgive us for the very thing that killed Him. What supreme love! What forgiveness! And now He expects, even commands, that we forgive others. I remind you that "others" does not just mean our brothers and sisters in the church, but it applies to our mates and our children as well. Anger, bitterness, resentment and hurt all require forgiveness. Paul admonished the Ephesians, "Get rid of all bitterness, rage and anger, brawling and slander, along with every form of malice. Be kind and compassionate to one another, forgiving each other, just as in Christ God forgave you" (Ephesians 4:31, 32).

He also told the folks in Colosse, "Bear with each other and forgive whatever grievances you may have against one another. Forgive as the Lord forgave you" (Colossians 3:13).

There is no mystery in these scriptures. The truth is plain and simple:

1. Bear with each other.

2. Get rid of all anger and bitterness.

3. Do not speak evil.

4. Be kind and tenderhearted.

5. Forgive just as Christ has forgiven you.

Practicing forgiveness in the family is to live in obedience to God's Word. Obedience is a prerequisite for spiritual renewal.

What God Thinks of an Unforgiving Spirit

A sobering Scripture passage will help remind us of just how important it is to follow the pattern of God's forgiveness. We must not violate this pattern as the unforgiving debtor did in Matthew 18:23-35. Even though he was forgiven for much, he chose not to forgive. Here's how the ending of this parable goes:

> "I canceled all that debt of yours because you begged me to. Shouldn't you have had mercy on your fellow servant just as I had on you?" In anger his master turned him over to the jailers to be tortured, until he should pay back all he owed. This is how my heavenly Father will treat each of you unless you forgive your brother from your heart.

This parable reinforces the pattern of forgiving others as God has forgiven us. That's the pattern, but how often are we required to obey it? Peter asked this question of Jesus immediately preceding this parable: "Lord, how many times shall I forgive my brother when he sins against me? Up to seven times?" Jesus replied, "I tell you, not seven times, but seventy-seven times" (vv. 21, 22).

When I am sitting at a restaurant with my family waiting for food, I usually play some kind of game with my two daughters. Often a teachable moment pops up that will help redeem the time.

One evening, we were playing a game where I started a Bible verse and my daughters took turns finishing it (a sentence completion quiz). One went like this: "Regarding forgiveness, Jesus said that we should not just forgive seven times but that we should forgive . . ." My youngest daughter, Amber, finished the sentence by saying, "Seventy times a day." Well, that's not quite what the Bible says, but it sure is at the heart of what it means. The literal interpretation does not mean that we should forgive 490 times ("seventy times seven," KJV) and then blast 'em. There is no time limit. Forgiving one another must be as limitless as God's forgiveness is to us.

One of the greatest hindrances to stability in family relationships is the inability or unwillingness to forgive past hurts. If you think you have forgiven, but your attitude toward your mate or children continues to be influenced by memories of past offenses, you haven't truly forgiven.

Dr. James Dobson once said, "A good marriage is not one where perfection reigns; it is a relationship where a healthy perspective overlooks a multitude of 'unresolvables.'"[2]

There may be issues in family relationships that are unresolvable, but as children of God we can agree to love and forgive each other in spite of our differences. We must choose to forgive, because we have been forgiven. The following comparison by Intimate Life Ministries gives insight into the common excuses given for not forgiving:

Common Excuse	Accurate Perception
The offender hasn't asked for forgiveness.	Forgiveness is for my benefit; I shouldn't wait.
The offender hasn't changed.	What if God waited for me to change before forgiving me?
The offender doesn't "deserve" forgiveness.	Who does "deserve" forgiveness?
Punishment is appropriate . . . and I'm going to do it.	"Vengeance is mine, says the Lord."
It's my right to hold a grudge.	Holding grudges hurts me, not the offender.
I'll forgive when I feel like it.	Forgiving is primarily a choice, not a feeling.

We need to deal immediately with misunderstandings, hurts, and anything else that would cause anger. Unresolved anger usually leads to negative emotions such as bitterness, fear, guilt, condemnation and despair. It may eventually affect us in physiological ways such as insomnia, high blood pressure, anxiety and headaches. Since there are no "perfect relationships," all relationships will inevitably produce some hurt. Our reluctance to deal with anger and conflict properly causes us to internalize negative emotions that God never intended for us to bear.[3] We are not only to forgive properly, but we are to forgive promptly.

Paul warns us, " 'In your anger do not sin': Do not let the sun go down while you are still angry" (Ephesians 4:26).

Syndicated columnist Ann Landers offers a healthy word of warning to deal with problems quickly.

She says, "One of the secrets of a long and fruitful life is to forgive everybody, everything, every night before you go to bed."[4]

It's a trick of Satan, the enemy of our soul and family, to get us to allow bitterness and anger to build up in our relationships. When this occurs, unforgiveness is usually the root of the problem. Someone has said: "Conflict is inevitable, but combat is optional." It is not *if* there is going to be conflicts in marriage and family relationships, but it is *how* we handle them — if we choose to forgive.

One of the smartest ways to avoid this trap is to deal with the issue quickly, using gentle words. Proverbs 15:1 gives good instruction on how to avoid anger and conflict: "A gentle answer turns away wrath, but a harsh word stirs up anger." Unresolved conflict has no place in God's pattern of forgiveness. God's command is crystal clear: "But if you do not forgive men their sins, your Father will not forgive your sins" (Matthew 6:15). God did not mince words on this topic; if we do not forgive, we will not be forgiven. We must practice forgiveness in order to avoid developing an unforgiving spirit.

FORGIVENESS IS A CHOICE

Forgiveness should be a way of life, not something you practice only when you feel like it. It's not a feeling, but a choice. Obviously our emotions are involved, but forgiveness must be based on more than emotions. If we're making a decision on emotional impulse, forgiveness may only last as

long as we have that feeling of emotion. Real forgiveness is a rational decision based on spiritual
values, Biblical admonition and God's example.
He forgave us, therefore we should forgive.

Humanly, it is difficult to forgive, especially
when you have to initiate forgiveness. It has been
said, "To err is human, but to forgive is divine." It
is much easier to forgive if we remind ourselves
that we have been forgiven. That's the pattern of
God's forgiveness.

One important aspect of this pattern is that we
practice forgiving unconditionally. We cannot
retrieve and rehearse those things we have forgiv-
en. Forgiveness after God's example promises not
to remember and retaliate! Joey Adams explains
this in *More Than Redemption*:

> Forgiveness is a promise. When God forgives
> a sinner, He does not simply become emo-
> tional over his repentance. No, instead, He
> goes on record that He has forgiven by mak-
> ing (and keeping) a promise to that effect:
> "Your sins and iniquities will I remember
> against you no more" (Jeremiah 31:34).

Dr. Adams goes on to define forgiveness as "a
formal declaration to lift the burden of one's guilt
and a promise to remember another's wrong
against him no more."[5]

Suzanne's story is a remarkable example of true
forgiveness. Now a grown woman, she was 18
when she lost her virginity.

The news crushed her parents. "When I saw their faces," she remembers, "I wanted to die. If only I could have undone it." Suzanne was prepared for anything—except forgiveness.

"We all cried together," she says, "but I'll never forget what happened after I went to bed that night. My dad crept into my room, bent down, and kissed me on the forehead. He actually kissed me. It was the most incredible feeling." Her parents' forgiveness was a turning point in her life. "If they could forgive me, I knew their love—and their religion—was real."[6]

Never are we to minimize the seriousness of sin, but we need to understand God's command to forgive it. We cannot arbitrarily pick and choose what sins we are willing to forgive. God doesn't. His love knows no bounds. Neither can we.

PRACTICE FORGIVENESS
The Biblical pattern is to . . .

- Forgive as you have been forgiven.

- Forgive as often as necessary.

- Forgive unconditionally.

The way to do this is to *choose* to forgive and then to *practice* that forgiveness. Regardless of the offense, there are four steps we can take that lead to forgiveness God's way:

1. *Decide* that you are going to forgive. Forgiveness is a choice. It is a rational decision not based solely on emotion. Choose to forgive unconditionally.

2. *Demonstrate* your forgiveness. Mental assertion or mere words will not do when it comes to forgiveness. We must show forgiveness in our behavior and demonstrate love and forgiveness in our daily lifestyle.

3. *Depend* on God to help you forgive. Renew your mind with new thoughts and attitudes. Even if you do remember the offense that has been forgiven doesn't mean that it must travel from your memory to your mouth. When the thought of the offense comes, immediately ask God to help you forget it. Replace the hurt with kind thoughts. Then forget it!

4. *Develop* ways to model and teach forgiveness in your family. "Joy unspeakable and full of glory" (1 Peter 1:8, KJV) comes as we imitate Christ's humility. A humble spirit leads to tenderness and forgiveness. Listen to these words from an old letter:

> If you have any encouragement from being united with Christ, if any comfort from his love, if any fellowship with the Spirit, if any tenderness and compassion, then make my joy complete by being like-minded, having the same love, being one in spirit and purpose. Do nothing out of selfish ambition or vain conceit, but in humility consider others better than yourselves. Each of you should look not only to your own interests, but also to the interests of others.

Your attitude should be the same as that of
Christ Jesus (Philippians 2:1-5).

He forgave!

One practical way to teach forgiveness in our
homes is to openly say, "I'm sorry." Pride keeps us
from apologizing to our mate or children. One of
the worst lies portrayed in *Love Story* is this line:
"Love means never having to say you are sorry."
Nothing could be further from the truth. One of the
most humbling and cleansing moments in my relationship with my family comes when I apologize
and ask for their forgiveness.

God's greatest gift was His Son, offered as a sacrifice, that we may be forgiven. We, in turn, have
the opportunity to practice forgiving others as God
has forgiven us. This awesome privilege must be
practiced with those we love the most—our family.
Nothing strengthens relationships more. Forgiveness breaks down walls of anger and resentment
that separate husbands and wives, parents and children. It brings inexpressible joy. We see this clearly
when David contemplates the goodness and forgiveness of God:

Praise the Lord, O my soul; all my inmost
being, praise his holy name. Praise the Lord,
O my soul, and forget not all his benefits—
who forgives all your sins and heals all your
diseases, who redeems your life from the pit
and crowns you with love and compassion,
who satisfies your desires with good things
so that your youth is renewed like the eagle's.

. . . He does not treat us as our sins deserve or repay us according to our iniquities. For as high as the heavens are above the earth, so great is his love for those who fear him; as far as the east is from the west, so far has he removed our transgressions from us. (Psalm 103:1-5, 10-12).

8

Expressing Appreciation and Affirmation

Words are powerful! Paul L. Walker masterfully portrays this in an article in *The Church of God Evangel*:

> Think about words! Words have started wars, destroyed character, built businesses, and inspired music, poetry and art. Without a doubt, one of the most powerful forces in the world is the power of words.
>
> Because of words, Patrick Henry was called the Voice of Revolution, Abraham Lincoln was called the Great Emancipator, and Winston Churchill was called the Statesman of the Century. Yet Jesus Christ spoke words that burned into the hearts of men.
>
> His words were imperishable: "My words will by no means pass away" (Mark 13:31).

His words were gracious: "So all bore witness to Him, and marveled at the gracious words which proceeded out of His mouth" (Luke 4:22).

His words were spiritual: "The words that I speak to you are spirit, and they are life" (John 6:63).

His words were life-giving: "Lord . . . You have the words of eternal life" (6:68).

His words were incomparable: "No man ever spoke like this Man!" (7:46).

His words were divine: "The word which you hear is not Mine but the Father's who sent Me" (14:24).

Now, what about our words? . . . Do we really understand the importance of our use of words? Christ said, "For by you words you will be justified, and by your words you will be condemned" (Matthew 12:37).

Words curse or bless, enslave or liberate, destroy or edify. Such is the power of our words that they are a window on our souls and the measure of our life in the Spirit.[1]

THE POWER OF WORDS

The power of the tongue can heal or harm family relationships. It can help build a strong family, or it can help destroy it. There is awesome power in the tongue. In comparison to other members of the body, it is small but so powerful. The Bible gives strong warning about its use:

> When we put bits into the mouths of horses to make them obey us, we can turn the whole animal. Or take ships as an example. Although they are so large and are driven by strong winds, they are steered by a very small rudder wherever the pilot wants to go. Likewise the tongue is a small part of the body, but it makes great boasts. Consider that a great forest is set on fire by a small spark. The tongue also is a fire, a world of evil among the parts of the body. It corrupts the whole person, sets the whole course of his life on fire, and is itself set on fire by hell (James 3:3-6).

The tongue is barely the width of your little finger, but it can move mountains. As seen in these scriptures, the tongue is compared to a horse's bridle, a rudder and a spark. A horse's bridle is so small, yet it controls such a large beast. A rudder is relatively small compared to the huge ship that it can direct. A spark is so tiny, but it can be responsible for destroying thousands of acres of forests.

David said, "Set a guard over my mouth, O Lord; keep watch over the door of my lips" (Psalm 141:3). The wisest man who ever lived said, "The Lord detests lying lips, but he delights in men who are truthful" (Proverbs 12:22).

Growing up, I often heard and probably recited the clever saying, "Sticks and stones may break my bones, but words will never hurt me." Not true—words do hurt. They cause pain that hangs around our neck like an albatross. In family relationships, words have incredible power to emotionally build up or tear down. Many of us remember words of praise our parents or spouse spoke to us years ago. I'm also sure that we can remember the negative, hurtful words spoken to us as well.

While I was writing this chapter, I decided to put this to the test. I tried to think back to my past to see if there were specific words spoken to me that still encourage or discourage me. I immediately thought of a positive comment that was shared with me 17 years ago relative to a spiritual giftedness in a certain area of my life. That one comment encouraged me to develop that gift in my life. I've done that and I believe that I have been an instrument of God's peace. The ripple effect of this person's kind words almost two decades ago has touched countless lives since.

Once words are spoken, you cannot take them back. I remember hearing a story a long time ago about a church member who came to her pastor and confessed for saying bad things about another church member. She wanted to know how to undo the damage she had created. The pastor told her to take a huge feather pillow to the top of the tallest building and let all of the feathers fly into the wind to be scattered east, west, north and south. He then instructed her to try to collect all of the feathers. It is just as impossible to "unspeak" words we have spoken and undo their damage.

Jim Weidman illustrated this during a family night object lesson by giving each of his children a tube of toothpaste and a paper plate. He instructed them to empty the toothpaste onto the paper plates any way they wanted to, making faces, towers or whatever. After they emptied the tubes, he gave each one of them a plastic spoon and drinking straw. He then placed a $20 bill on the table and told them that the first one to get all of the toothpaste back into the tube would get $20. After several minutes of scooping and cramming toothpaste, sucking it up with straws, and trying to blow it into the tubes, they finally gave up. The father knew that his $20 bill was safe. Just like it was impossible to put toothpaste back into the tubes, it is impossible to "unspeak" words.

Your family desperately needs to hear words of comfort, affirmation, encouragement and praise from you on a regular basis. Words that build up are like rays of sunshine. They encourage, edify, and lift up our spirits. As a member of a Christian family, we need to be seriously aware of our spoken words and the power that they possess.

Withholding Words of Blessing

We also need to be aware of how powerful the *absence* of spoken words can be. It is not good enough to just guard our lips and not say damaging, negative words, but we must be proactive and bless our family members with loving, positive words.

Dr. Howard Hendricks, noted author and Christian educator tells the story of a couple he counseled with several years ago. The couple had been married more than 20 years, but they were considering getting a divorce. Dr. Hendricks asked the husband when was the last time he told his wife that he loved her. After some thought and nervous agitation he said, "On my wedding day I told my wife that I loved her, and it stands until I revoke it!"

This gave a good clue to what was destroying this marriage. When we withhold words of blessings in our family relationships, we fail to meet their needs of security, appreciation, acceptance and approval. Anything that we don't feed dies. Our family relationships need to be fed a daily dose of love, affirmation, appreciation and encouragement. Our spouses and children need it and deserve it. "Do not withhold good from those who deserve it, when it is in your power to act. Do not say to your neighbor, 'Come back later; I'll give it tomorrow' — when you now have it with you" (Proverbs 3:27, 28).

"In" With the Positive

I probably should explain why I am writing about the positive first and then about the negative in the next section. It may appear that ending on a positive note would be better. But the reason is obvious. Filling our conversation with positive,

encouraging words will either drive out the negative or never allow it to take a foothold in the first
place. I've heard it said that we don't sing because
we are happy, but we're happy because we sing. If
we wait until we are happy to sing, it could be a
long time. It's much better to go ahead and sing
anyway—happiness will come. Focus on the positive and watch the negative flee.

A positive climate helps create positive people.
And positive people are contagious, because optimism breeds optimism. Recently, I heard someone
say that an optimist is a person who will go after
Moby Dick in a rowboat and take along the tartar
sauce. However, what we need in our families goes
beyond optimistic thinking. We need to spend
enough time with God in prayer and feed on His
Holy Word, so that we can bless our family with
words of love and encouragement. This is the
wonderful instruction given in Ephesians 4:29: "Do
not let any unwholesome talk come out of your
mouths, but only what is helpful for building others up according to their needs, that it may benefit
those who listen."

Now there is a scripture to live by! It goes
beyond selfishness and pie-in-the-sky optimism.
Here is a story I found over 10 years ago:

> Larry and Jo Ann were an ordinary couple.
> They lived in an ordinary house on an ordi-
> nary street. Like other ordinary couples, they
> struggled to make ends meet and to do the
> right things for their children.

They were ordinary in yet another way; they had their squabbles. Much of their conversation concerned what was wrong in their marriage and who was to blame. Until one day, when the most extraordinary event took place.

"You know, Jo Ann, I've got a magic chest of drawers. Every time I open them, they're full of socks and underwear," Larry said. "I want to thank you for filling them all these years."

Jo Ann stared at her husband over the top of her spectacles. "What do you want, Larry?"

"Nothing. I just want you to know I appreciate those magic drawers."

This wasn't the first time Larry had done something odd, so Jo Ann pushed the incident out of her mind until a few days later.

"Jo Ann, thank you for recording so many correct check numbers in the ledger this month. You put down the right number fifteen out of sixteen times. That's a record."

Disbelieving what she heard, Jo Ann looked up from her mending: "Larry, you're always complaining about my recording the wrong check numbers. Why stop now?"

"No reason. I just wanted you to know I appreciate the effort you're making."

Jo Ann shook her head and went back to her mending. "What's gotten into him?" she mumbled.

Nevertheless, the next day when Jo Ann wrote a check at the grocery store, she glanced at the checkbook to confirm that she had put down the right check number. "Why do I suddenly care about those dumb numbers?" she asked herself. She tried to disregard the incident, but Larry's strange behavior intensified.

"Jo Ann, that was a great dinner," he said one evening. "I appreciate all your effort. Why, in the past fifteen years I'll bet you've prepared over 14,000 meals for me and the kids."

"Gee, Jo Ann, the house looks great. You've really worked hard to get it looking so good." And even, "Thanks, Jo Ann, for just being you. I really enjoy your company."

Jo Ann was growing worried. "Where's the sarcasm, the criticism," she wondered. Her fears that something peculiar was happening to her husband were confirmed by 16-year-old Shelly, who complained, "Dad's gone bonkers, Mom. He just told me I looked nice. With all this makeup and these sloppy clothes, he still said it. That's not like Dad. What's wrong with him?"

Whatever was wrong, Larry didn't get over

it. Day in and day out he continued focusing on the positive. Over the weeks, Jo Ann grew more used to her mate's unusual behavior, and occasionally even gave him a grudging "thank you." She prided herself in taking it all in stride, until one day something so peculiar happened she became completely discombobulated:

"I want you to take a break," Larry said. "I am going to do the dishes. So please take your hands off that frying pan and leave the kitchen." (Long, long pause.) "Thank you, Larry. Thank you very much!"

Jo Ann's step was now a little light, her self-confidence higher, and once in a while she hummed. She didn't seem to experience blue moods much anymore. "I rather like Larry's new behavior," she thought.

That would have been the end of the story except one day, another most extraordinary event took place. This time it was Jo Ann who spoke.

"Larry," she said, "I want to thank you for going to work and providing for us all these years. I don't think I've ever told you how much I appreciate it."

Larry has never revealed the reason for his dramatic change of behavior no matter how

hard Jo Ann has pushed for an answer, and
so it will likely remain one of life's mysteries.
But it's one I'm thankful to live with. You see,
I am Jo Ann.[2]

Jo Ann needed to be appreciated and affirmed. I
believe her husband understood that "a good
word" would help meet her needs. In doing so, he
was building her up—meeting her needs.

Ephesians 4:29 is one of those jewels in Scripture
that plays out extremely well in everyday life.
Focusing on the positive and sharing words of appreciation possesses the power to change the climate of
our home, our attitudes and our personalities. A positive home is not just a place to eat and sleep, but it is
a place to develop healthy views of life and godly
character.   In her famous poem, "Children Learn
What They Live," Dorothy Law Nolte suggests:

> If a child lives with encouragement, he learns
>   to be confident.
> If a child lives with tolerance, he learns to be
>   patient.
> If a child lives with praise, he learns to be
>   appreciative.
> If a child lives with acceptance, he learns to love.
> If a child lives with approval, he learns to like
>   himself.
> If a child lives with recognition, he learns it is
>   good to have a goal.
> If a child lives with sharing, he learns about
>   generosity.

If a child lives with honesty and fairness, he
    learns what truth and justice are.
If a child lives with security, he learns to have
    faith in himself and in those about him.
If a child lives with friendliness, he learns that
    the world is a nice place in which to live.
If a child lives with serenity, your child will
    live with peace of mind.

May it be so in our families and in our marriages.

"OUT" WITH THE NEGATIVE

Have you ever been around someone so negative that when they walk into a room, the
lights go dim? They remind me of the wife who
was so negative that her husband was bound
and determined to show her something she
could be positive about. So one day he took her
out to a lake to duck-hunt with his new dog.
When the ducks flew, he shot one that landed in
the middle of the lake. Immediately, his new
dog ran out, walking on the water, to retrieve
the duck. When the dog returned to the shore,
the husband turned to his wife and said, "Now,
what do you think about that?" fully expecting
a positive comment. But she replied, "What's
the matter, can't the dog swim?"

I have not met many negative people who were
happy. A negative spirit is usually an indication of
a deeper spiritual problem that will eventually be
manifested. Here is a sample of how God feels
about the problem:

When words are many, sin is not absent, but he who holds his tongue is wise (Proverbs 10:19).

A quarrelsome wife is like a constant dripping on a rainy day; restraining her is like restraining the wind or grasping oil with the hand (Proverbs 27:15, 16).

As charcoal to embers and as wood to fire, so is a quarrelsome man for kindling strife (Proverbs 26:21).

Never criticize or condemn—or it will all come back on you (Luke 6:37, *TLB*).

It is much easier to be negative and critical than to be positive and encouraging. If we could see the destructive effects of criticism, I think we would think twice before speaking a discouraging word. Satan wants to destroy our families. He is the expert on condemning, judging, criticizing and blaming. As a matter of fact, the Bible characterizes him as our vicious Enemy, prowling around "like a hungry, roaring lion, looking for some victim to tear apart" (1 Peter 5:8, *TLB*). That's exactly what critical words do—tear at our being.

In our day-to-day family living, Robert Fisher states that we could characterize nagging as "gnawing or nibbling." However, negative criticism would better be described as "biting and devouring."[3] That's exactly what the apostle Paul writes about in Galatians: "The entire law is summed up in a single command: 'Love your neighbor as yourself.' If you

keep on biting and devouring each other, watch out
or you will be destroyed by each other" (5:14, 15). *The
Living Bible* translates verse 15 this way: "But if
instead of showing love among yourselves you are
always critical and catty, watch out! Beware of ruin-
ing each other."

In Ephesians 4:29, we are encouraged to not tear
anybody down with our words but to build them
up. It is so important for us to build each other up.
In 2:10, Paul explained, "For we are God's work-
manship, created in Christ Jesus to do good works,
which God prepared in advance for us to do."

Every family member is created in the image of
God, worthy of honor, respect, kind words and
encouragement. Jean Fleming, in *A Mother's Heart*,
asks a good question:

> A sentence from Psalm 101 has been both chal-
> lenging and convicting for me. "I will walk in
> my house with blameless heart" (Psalm 101:2,
> *NIV*). When God speaks to me about being
> more loving, this verse reminds me to make
> application in my family first—and then to
> others. It forces me to ask, "Am I more spiritu-
> al, more loving, or more fun somewhere else?
> Who gets my best—my family or others?"[4]

I will now finish Dorothy Law Nolte's poem,
"Children Learn What They Live":

> If a child lives with criticism, he learns to condemn.
> If a child lives with hostility, he learns to fight.
> If a child lives with fear, he learns to be apprehensive.

If a child lives with pity, he learns to feel sorry for
himself.
If a child lives with ridicule, he learns to be shy.
If a child lives with jealousy, he learns what envy is.
If a child lives with shame, he learns to feel guilty.

I have heard it said that children need at least seven positive statements, or affirmations, to erase one negative. That should serve as a guide for our daily communication with our families.

Negative words and criticism cause resentment and pain that last a lifetime. The Bible is adamant about God's people speaking words of encouragement and edification rather than negative words of criticism. This applies to our marriage and family first!

Let us be challenged to a godly lifestyle by this passage in Romans:

> You have no right to criticize your brother or look down on him. Remember, each of us will stand personally before the Judgment Seat of God. For it is written, "As I live," says the Lord, "every knee shall bow to me and every tongue confess to God." Yes, each of us will give an account of himself to God. So don't criticize each other any more (14:10-13, *TLB*).

In with the good and out with the bad!

AFFIRMATION AND APPRECIATION

Most people love to be praised. Your spouse and

children are no exception. Mark Twain said, "I can live for two months on a good compliment." King Solomon noted the affect of compliments in Proverbs 12:25: "An anxious heart weighs a man down, but a kind word cheers him up." Compliments, words of appreciation and affirmation are powerful communicators of love. Professor William James of Harvard said it years ago, "The deepest principle in human nature is the craving to be appreciated."[5]

"One thing scientists have discovered," notes Theodore Dreier, "is that often-praised children become more intelligent than often-blamed ones. There's a creative element in praise."[6]

In 1 Thessalonians 5:11, the apostle Paul said, "Therefore encourage one another and build each other up." Scriptural admonition like this is not just for the church, but for the home as well. It would be an excellent and Biblical idea for us to give our spouse and each of our children at least one compliment per day. Why not just go ahead and commit right now to do that for the next 21 days. It may be habit-forming. The experts say that it takes 21 days to form a new habit. Breaking a bad habit is great, but replacing it with a good habit is even better. Here is another suggestion: There are four times in each day that are wonderful opportunities to enrich family relationships. A positive word of affirmation or appreciation at these four "impression points" can be powerful in building strong loving relationships with your spouse and children. Watch for them and apply a daily dose of affirmation and appreciation:

1. The first words that you say to your spouse and children as you awake in the mornings

2. The last words that you say to each other as you leave each other going to work or school

3. The first words that you say to each other when you gather back together after work or school

4. The last words that you say to each other before you retire for sleep at night.

These are times that are memorable and will help build loving relationships through affirmation and appreciation. Proverbs 25:11 declares, "A word aptly spoken is like apples of gold in settings of silver."

We need to look for opportunities to express love and appreciation. Jack Canfield in his best-selling book, *Chicken Soup for the Soul*, illustrates the importance of showing appreciation and its role in building family relationships:

> One dad writes a Post-it note to his daughter every night before he goes to bed. He puts it in a place where she will be sure to find it in the morning—on her mirror, in her lunch box, on her bedroom door, or in some other conspicuous place. On each note he writes something he appreciates about her. "I appreciated your help with the dishes tonight," or "I was really inspired by how hard you worked on your math and got an A on your final."

One day he went into her room looking for a lost hammer. On his way out he saw 250 Post-it notes stuck on the back of her bedroom door. His daughter had kept every one of his notes. So now, every time she leaves her bedroom she sees 250 notes of appreciation that remind her that somebody loves her. What a powerful message! What wonderful affirmation! All from a simple Post-it note.[7]

Jerry and Jack Schreur share the following results of two studies that pinpoint the power of affirmation.

In one, Delores Curran, noted authority on family, asked 500 professionals who work with families and asked them to list the traits of a healthy family. Of 56 traits listed by the respondents, second on the list was "appreciation."

In another, David More, a marriage and family specialist, found in several studies that "affirming" one another is the common thread that runs through all happy families. The studies also revealed that the members of these families liked each other and were open about expressing their affections. The natural result of this was that the family enjoyed being with each other and enjoyed reinforcing each other. Family relationships were very affirming and satisfying.[8] This is graphically portrayed in the family of Gail MacDonald:

Once, when our children were about 5 and 8, they were caught arguing. I can remember my husband stopping them and saying, "This is home. Now, outside of these four walls people are going to hurt you, they're going to call you names. But inside these four walls we build each other. Do you understand? We build each other."

And that became a by-word in our home. Are you building? Many times when Gordon or I would say something derogatory to each other, the children would say, "Mother, was that a building comment?" When everybody gets on the building bandwagon, it makes a big difference.[9]

God's heart is touched when He sees us loving and building up one another with our appreciation and affirmation.

SPEAK THE TRUTH ... IN LOVE

I heard about a pastor who preached on the subject of hell every week. His church members grew tired of his sermons and wanted him to resign. Eventually he did. Their new pastor arrived and his first sermon was on the subject of hell. He continued to preach on hell every Sunday and the congregation loved him. What was the difference? The first pastor preached on hell like he wanted them to go there. The second preacher preached on hell like he wanted to keep them *from* going there. Same subject, but different motivation. Most of the time it's not what we do, it's *how* we do it. It's not what we say, it's *how* we say it.

Instead, speaking the truth in love, we will in all things grow up into him who is the Head, that is, Christ. . . . Therefore each of you must put off falsehood and speak truthfully to his neighbor, for we are all members of one body (Ephesians 4:15, 25).

These verses tell us two things: Always speak the truth and always speak the truth motivated by love.

First, we are told *what* to speak. There is never an acceptable time to be anything less than honest. Lying is a sin. So we must always tell the truth when we speak. But the crucial decision is *when* you should speak. Just because something is true does not mean you have to speak it. Suppose that while sitting in my living room, I look over at my youngest daughter and say, "I noticed earlier today when you were playing that you looked clumsy and uncoordinated." Would that really bless her and make her day? No, the spirit of that scripture is in the second part—"in love."

Therefore, it is extremely important *how* we speak. We need to speak the truth *in love*. Think about this principle against the backdrop of 1 Corinthians 13. If we must speak the truth "in love," what does it really mean? This is how Paul details its nature (vv. 4-8):

Love is patient,
    love is kind.
It does not envy,
    it does not boast,
    it is not proud.

It is not rude,
    it is not self-seeking,
    it is not easily angered,
    it keeps no record of wrongs.
Love does not delight in evil
    but rejoices with the truth.
It always protects,
    always trusts,
    always hopes,
    always perseveres.
Love never fails.

9

Times, Traditions and Teachable Moments

Imagine a bank that credits your account each morning with $86,400. It carries over no balance from day to day. Every morning it deletes whatever part of the balance you failed to use during the day. What would you do? Draw out every cent? Of course!

Each of us has such a bank. Its name is *time*. Every morning, it credits you with 86,400 seconds. Every night it writes off, as lost, all you have failed to use. It carries over no balance. It allows no overdraft.

Each day it opens a new account for you. Each night it burns the remains of the day. If you fail to use the day's deposits, the loss is yours. There is no going back. There is no drawing against the "tomorrow." You must live in the present on today's deposits. Invest it so as to get from it the utmost in health,

happiness, and success! The clock is running.
Make the most of today.

To realize the value of ONE YEAR, ask a stu-
    dent who failed a grade.
To realize the value of ONE MONTH, ask a
    mother who gave birth to a premature baby.
To realize the value of ONE WEEK, ask the
    editor of the weekly newspaper.
To realize the value of ONE HOUR, ask the
    couple in love who is waiting to meet.
To realize the value of ONE MINUTE, ask a
    person who missed the train.
To realize the value of ONE SECOND, ask a
    person who just avoided an accident.
To realize the value of ONE MILLISECOND,
    ask the person who won a silver medal in
    the Olympics.

Treasure every moment that you have! And
treasure it more because you shared it with
someone special, special enough to spend
your time. And remember that time waits
for no one.

Yesterday is history.
Tomorrow is mystery.
Today is a gift . . . that's why it's called the
    present![1]

   Cash, cars, homes, college tuition, diamonds,
clothes—nothing is as precious and priceless to your
family as the time you give them. To withhold the

precious gift of time could have destructive results.

A runaway teenager wrote these words to her family back home:

Dear Folks,

Thank you for everything, but I am going to Chicago and try to start some kind of a new life.

You asked me why I did those things and why I gave you so much trouble, and the answer is easy for me to give you, but I am wondering if you will understand.

Remember when I was just about six or seven and I used to want you to just listen to me? I remember all the nice things you gave me for Christmas and my birthday and I was really happy with the things—for about a week—at the time I got the things, but the rest of the time during the year I really didn't want presents. I just wanted all the time for you to listen to me like I was somebody who felt things too, because I remember even when I was young, I felt things. But you said you were busy.

If anybody asks you where I am, tell them I've gone looking for somebody with time because I've got a lot of things I want to talk about.[2]

Paul left us practical instruction about this gift of time: "See then that ye walk circumspectly, not as fools, but as wise, redeeming the time, because the days are evil" (Ephesians 5:15, 16, KJV).

So let's think about it, parents. What have we established as priorities? Where does our marital relationship and relationships with our children rank in order of these priorities?

LOVE IS SPELLED T-I-M-E

Fifteen hundred school children were recently asked, "What do you think makes a happy home?" It was refreshing to see what they did not place high on their lists. One would think that TV, money, video games and such would be at the top of the list. The answer, however, they gave most frequently was "Doing things together."[3]

Steve Farrar relates the following story about Dr. Robert Schuller:

> A number of years ago, he was on a whirlwind book-promotion tour, visiting eight cities in four days. It was an exhausting schedule, in addition to the normal duties Dr. Schuller had on his shoulder as pastor of a large church. As he was going over his return schedule with his secretary, she reminded him that he was scheduled to have lunch with the winner of a charity raffle. Tickets had been raffled for a lunch with Dr. Schuller. Schuller was suddenly sobered when he found out that the $500 bid to have lunch with him represented that person's entire life savings. He knew this because the person who was willing to spend $500 to have lunch with him was his own teenage daughter. Dr. Schuller obviously loves his

family. (He graciously allowed Paul Harvey to tell this story in his column). It simply reminds us that we can be so busy doing good that we forget what is really important.[4]

Not long ago, Gary Baurer, author of *Our Journey Home*, testified before the House Select Committee on Children, Youth and Families. Gary tells us what happened:

> The committee chairwoman had arranged for a 12-year-old kid, who plays on a Nickelodeon television show, to appear as one of its "star" witnesses. The idea was to use this child actor's appearance before this congressional panel to attract media attention and give some members of the committee and their carefully coached 12-year-old accomplice, a chance to call for "children's rights," more day care, and other "progressive" ideas that the experts in Washington think will solve our problems.
>
> But Congressman Clyde Holloway rained on the committee's parade that day. With the cameras rolling and the crowded hearing room hanging on each word, the Louisiana Republican turned to the 12-year-old boy and asked, "If you could be king for a day, how would you spend your time?"
>
> Caught off-guard by this unscripted inquiry, the child actor did a funny thing. With refreshing candor, he answered as I suspect most kids

would. He said if he were king for a day, he'd
want to spend his day at Disney World or at
some other location filled with childhood
amusements. He'd want to eat lots of ice
cream and candy bars and stay up late. But
most of all, he said he'd want to spend his day
with his family, with his mom and dad,
because between their busy work schedules,
they never really spent enough time together.[5]

What these stories have in common is the notion
that nothing replaces time spent together as a family. Equally important is spending quality time as a
couple. The cornerstone of a strong family is built
on a strong marital relationship.

In America, divorce rates, fractured families and
dysfunctional family relationships are at an all-time
high. A hundred years ago, about 54 percent of a
family's waking hours was time spent together.
Today, that percentage has dropped to about 18 percent. Is it any wonder that families are becoming
fragmented? I'm aware of new demands placed on
families that increase workload, travel, school and
civic involvements. Justified or not, the results are
the same. It takes time to nurture and develop strong
marital and family relationships. Today's cultural
demands are different, but there are ways to carve
out time for our family. Watching less TV and playing fewer computer games is one way. Some experts
estimate that the average child in America will
watch 30,000 to 40,000 television commercials per
year. That's entirely possible since the average TV

set in America is on several hours per day and serves as an electronic parent to many children.

As I was writing this chapter, I read an article in the *Cleveland Daily Banner* about professionals who are working less, but who still succeed.   Here is a portion of that article:

> Charlotte Hawthorne advanced her high-powered career with Eli Lilly and Co. by working fewer hours and spending more time with her family. Sound like a pipe dream? Researchers at Indiana's Purdue University and Montreal's McGill University say that in many large North American corporations, that dream has become reality. In fact, some corporations predict that customizing work arrangements — which help employees balance careers and family life — will be the key to managing the modern work force.[6]

Major corporations are seeing the need for families to spend time together. Generally we find time for the things that are important to us. What is more important than your family? Josh McDowell shares a sad commentary of what happens when we don't make time for family:

> Some of the saddest words that parents ever say is, "If only I had spent more time . . . if only I had listened to my kids more . . . if only . . ."
>
> The wife of a senior vice president of a huge construction firm heard Josh speak at a local

church about being available to your children. Later, Josh ran into the same woman in a restaurant. She mentioned hearing him talk, and then she started to cry.

"I have to share something with you," she said hesitantly. "My husband just died. He was a million-dollar-a-year man. He traveled all over the world building and constructing things, but he never took time for his children, even when he was home. All his children turned against him, and when they were grown, they would have nothing to do with him. On his deathbed he confessed to me that he was dying one of the saddest men in the world. He told me, 'I gained prestige, but I lost my family. If only I had spent more time with my children.'"[7]

Do not be cursed with the *if* word. I am reminded of the Scriptural admonition in Matthew 16:26, "What good will it be for a man if he gains the whole world, yet forfeits his soul? Or what can a man give in exchange for his soul?" A good family-oriented paraphrase would sound something like this: "What good will it be for parents or spouses to gain every honor and possession possible and yet forfeit their marriage and family in the process?"

QUALITY AND QUANTITY TIME

Some say that they don't have a lot of time (quantity) to spend with their family. There's a term for this I call "hogwash." It just doesn't work that way. During hours of quantity time come divine appointments and teachable moments called *quality time*. We cannot manufacture quality time. It is a myth to think that a few minutes of quality time here or there can make up for the lack of quantity time. Time is the precious commodity that provides the necessary framework for all areas of family health — value formation, communication, affirmation, service, teaching, modeling and relationship building.

The late Erma Bombeck, who is noted for her family-related humor, shared a touching story about her father who did not spend much time with his children.

> One morning my father didn't get up and go to work. He went to the hospital and died the next day.
>
> I hadn't thought that much about him before. He was just someone who left and came home and seemed glad to see everyone at night. He opened the jar of pickles when no one else could. He was the only one in the house who wasn't afraid to go into the basement by himself.
>
> He cut himself shaving, but no one kissed it or got excited about it. It was understood when it rained, he got the car and brought it around to the door. When anyone was sick, he went out to get the prescription filled. He took lots of pictures, but he was never in them.

Whenever I played house, the mother doll had a lot to do. I never knew what to do with the daddy doll, so I had him say, "I'm going off to work now," and threw him under the bed.

The funeral was in our living room and a lot of people came and brought all kinds of good food and cakes. We never had so much company before.

I went to my room and felt under my bed for the daddy doll. When I found him, I dusted him off and put him on my bed.

He never did anything. I didn't know his leaving would hurt so much.[8]

We don't have to be perfect parents, but we do need to be present parents. Even though we should never replace quantity time with a few minutes here and there of quality time, at the same time we must not forsake the value of real quality time.

Quality time means giving your spouse or child your undivided attention. It does not mean geographical presence. Being in the same house or same room with someone doesn't mean you're giving them your time and attention. A central characteristic of quality time is "togetherness." Togetherness means focused attention, wanting to be there and giving yourself to others. With a small child it may be sitting in the floor playing. For a teen it may mean attending a game or playing a game with them. To a spouse it may mean taking them out for a cup of coffee and only talking about them and their life.

Time is a gift from God we need to invest wisely. We should not kill time, or do time. Criminals can do that.

KILLING THE TIME KILLER

Ephesians 5:16 tells us to redeem the time and to be wise with the usage of our time. Is it possible to waste hours watching TV and still be obedient to the Scriptures? Statistics indicate that the average American family watches 7 to 12 hours of TV per day. Let's say that we, as Christian families, watch TV only three hours per day, less than half the national average. That still translates into more than 60,000 hours in a lifetime—more than seven years spent in front of the TV.

Families can create hours of quality family time that can be spent in activities, in prayer, in Bible study, or other Christian disciplines with a single click to the "off" button on the television or computer.

A fascinating experiment on "television addiction" was reported in *Good Housekeeping Magazine*. A Detroit newspaper made an offer of $500 to 120 families who would agree not to watch TV for one month. Unbelievably 93 families turned down the offer. Only 27 accepted the challenge. Of those 27 families, five were selected to be studied and a report prepared on their family behavior for that month. The results were amazing! Each family had been watching between 40 to 70 hours of television per week. For the entire month the TV was not turned on. Here's what happened:

- Books were taken off shelves and read that had never been touched.

- Children took baths earlier without even being told.

- Families sat around the living room talking about the events of each other's day.

- Homework was done without being told.

- Everyone got in bed at an earlier hour.

Four important results were shared by the "no-TV-month" families:

1. Their family members became closer.

2. There was more eyeball-to-eyeball time between parents and children.

3. There was "marked increase" in patience between family members.

4. Creativity was greatly enhanced.[9]

Think how spiritually renewing this would be!

Another red flag for killing time is computers, especially the Internet. Computers are becoming just as addictive and lethal as television. In my counseling with couples and families, I see the devastating results of involvement with the Internet. Pornography is so easily accessible and unregulated. I strongly encourage parents to secure the highest level of parental controls with Internet services. Beyond that, I also recommend limiting viewing time, regardless of the content. What a shameful waste of eternal moments. Remember, every hour spent on computers, TV and video games robs an hour that could be spent with your spouse and children.

FAMILY TRADITIONS

Family traditions are important in building strong, spiritual families. They provide a sense of identity. Family traditions are relational and spiritual touchstones that help us make memories we can pass down as a strong, spiritual heritage.

Mort Grimes, in *Let's Make a Memory*, tells of the impact of tradition:

> One of the traditions our family has carried on from my parents (and hopefully our children will pass it along to their children) is the custom of reading the lovely story of Jesus' birth from the Gospel of Luke before opening our Christmas presents.

> Grandparents, sisters, brothers, uncles, aunts, and cousins have all participated in this ritual over the years. Now, both grandfathers are gone, but how fortunate we are to have my father, Pop Crim, and Nicki's father, Pop Dale, on tape reading the Christmas story to

the family — which incidentally proved to be their last Christmas with us.

We think it is a beautiful tradition worth passing along to our children.[10]

Family traditions have the power to literally change your family's future. Tim Smith and Otis Ledbetter define family traditions as, "the practice of handing down stories, beliefs and customs from one generation to another in order to establish and reinforce a strong sense of identity."[11]

Ron Clarkson says it this way: "Healthy families believe in traditions. Traditions say to all of us, 'We did this in the past and we're doing it right now. We're going to do this year after year after year.' This provides a secret power of continuity and security in our homes."[12]

Investing time in family traditions today can create family togetherness and spiritual development for the future. And the more we sow, the more our family reaps. "Whoever sows sparingly will also reap sparingly, and whoever sows generously will also reap generously" (2 Corinthians 9:6).

The prophet Joel also had something to say about the significance of influencing the next generation:

Hear this, you elders; listen, all who live in the land. Has anything like this ever happened in your days of your forefathers? Tell it to your children, and let your children tell it to their children, and their children to the next generation (1:2, 3).

Even though Joel's message involved a warning to God's people, the central message is sound advice for influencing generations to come.

Traditions help us create memories for a lifetime. Edith Schaffer asks the question, "What is a family meant to be?" Among other things, I personally have always felt it is meant to be a museum of memories — collections of carefully preserved memories."[13]

Stephan Covey feels so strongly about their importance that he equates traditions as the essence of family renewal. In his book *7 Habits of a Highly Effective Family*, he writes:

> Family traditions include rituals and celebrations and meaningful events that you do in your family. They help you understand who you are: that you are part of a family that's a strong unit, that you love one another, that you respect and honor one another, that you celebrate one another's birthdays and special events, and make positive memories for everybody.

> Through traditions you reinforce the connection of the family. You give a feeling of belonging, of being supported, of being understood. You are committed to one another. You are a part of something that's greater than yourself. You express and show loyalty to one another. You need to be needed, you need to be wanted, and you're glad to be part of a family. When parents and children

cultivate traditions that are meaningful to them, every time they go back to that tradition it renews the emotional energy and bonding of the past.

These traditions—big or small—are the things that bond us, renew us and give us identity as a family.[14]

There seems to be a clear connection between strong families and family traditions. But like all things, all traditions are not helpful in establishing a sensitive, affectionate atmosphere that nurtures spiritual renewal in the home. Here are a few warning labels:

1. Traditions should not become boring, meaningless rituals.

2. Not every family tradition will be spiritual. Some are just fun things to do.

3. Traditions can be overused. Some traditions, like nightly prayer and memorizing Scripture, should be repeated. On the other hand, if your child likes "pizza night," you can overdo it by having it several nights a week. Some things are best when scheduled for special occasions.

Traditions have the power to mold, shape and direct families in many ways. They exert a remarkable influence on the lives of family members for generations to come.

Making Memories For a Lifetime

Meaningful family traditions are limited only by your imagination. The sky is the limit! There are different categories of traditions. Traditions could be daily, weekly, monthly or annual events. They may be organized around holidays. They can be traditions for couples or the entire family. Other traditions could involve birthdays, special events, reading times, table talk, festivals, fun times, milestone events, trips or religious events. What a smorgasbord of possibilities! Here is a list of what some families are doing:

- One mother and daughter kiss the palm of each other's hand every morning, close their hands tightly and put their hands in their pockets. During the day they can reach into their pockets, take out the kiss and plant it on their cheek.

- One father cooks breakfast every Saturday morning for the family, preparing a surprise menu item each week.

- One family exercises together every evening.

- One family video tapes Christmas morning every year and watches it the following Christmas Eve while enjoying popcorn balls and hot chocolate.

- One family goes bowling every New Year's Eve.

- Another family dresses up for Christmas

dinner, lights candles and reads the Christmas story.

Here are a few more ideas:

- Schedule a regular date with each child once a month.

- Keep a family diary on the coffee table and encouraging family members to write in it regularly, sharing special thoughts, God's grace and thankful comments.

- Have a time after church each Sunday for a "Second Sermon." Each family member shares insights on the morning message while driving home or over Sunday dinner.

- Have the family put together a jigsaw puzzle every Christmas, glue it together, frame it and start a puzzle gallery on a designated wall in the house.

- Celebrate one day of the year as "Children's Day." Celebrate it to the hilt just like Mother's Day or Father's Day.

- Have a family "group" hug before leaving for school or work each morning.

- Call a different relative on the phone on specific nights every week or month.

- Read a Bible verse before or after dinner.

- Say bedtime prayers with children each night.

Several years ago, Kathy and I taught in a Christian

school in Richmond, Virginia. We were so impressed with one of our families who designated every Friday night as Pizza Night. On Fridays, barring an emergency, it was pizza and games for the family. I still remember the three children and how excited they were every Friday, anticipating a night of pizza and games. Somehow, I really don't think it was all about cheap food and checkers. Deep down, they were drinking in the love of their parents and the bonding time as a family.

We have established many traditions over the years in my own home. One Thanksgiving, 14 years ago, our family decided to go up on Fort Mountain in Chatsworth, Georgia to a hotel and restaurant. Our extended families lived far away and we wanted to begin a family tradition of our own. The view was breathtaking, the food was wonderful and the atmosphere warm and cozy right down to the five-foot logs burning in the fireplace. Our 9-year-old son, Lee, wanted us all to gather around the table and share things for which we were thankful. We had a wonderful time.

My mother moved into a senior citizen complex behind the church where I minister. I told my son that I guess we would have to postpone or discontinue our trip to Fort Mountain for Thanksgiving because all of my brothers and sister would be coming to town. His response was a mix of humor and seriousness. "Oh, no dad, we've got to go. It's a family tradition. If we don't go, I'll be emotionally scarred for life." So we helped prepare food for my mother and dropped it off at her place on our way to Fort Mountain. And, of course, we ended up later at Moms' house for leftovers. This family tradition continues and it wouldn't surprise me if my children's families ended up atop Fort Mountain, Georgia on Thanksgiving Day.

Family traditions help you make memories for a lifetime. They can be fun, teach deep spiritual truths, encourage family members to pray and provide family identity.

Family Nights

There is one family tradition that is vital in every Christian home. Call it family devotions, family nights, family time or family worship—the important thing is that it is a family affair.

Ideally, families need a type of devotion every night, but I am certainly not going to heap guilt on you if you are not doing so. However, I do strongly encourage you to have a family night at least once a week. That's an achievable goal we can all work toward.

A major part of one evening a week set aside for "family night" will do wonders for your family. It will also create family unity and relationship building. Family nights give us a quality time each week to help our children develop a sense of self-worth, to have fun with them and a time to share words of affirmation. It is a powerful tool to use in helping make memories for a lifetime.

Don't wait! Start now! Time marches on and it's gone before we know it. I'm sure many of us can relate to the reality check described by Chuck Swindoll called "Someday":

> Someday when the kids are grown . . . things are going to be a lot different. The garage won't be full of bikes, unfinished "experimental projects," and the rabbit cage. I'll be able to park both cars neatly in just the right places, and never again stumble over skateboards or roller-skates.

> Someday when the kids are grown . . . the kitchen will be incredibly neat. The sink will be free of sticky dishes, the garbage disposal won't get choked on rubber bands or paper cups, and the refrigerator won't be clogged with nine bottles of milk.

> Someday when the kids are grown . . . the instrument called a "telephone" will actually be available. It won't look like it's growing from a teenager's ear. It will simply hang there . . . silently and amazingly available! It will be free of lipstick, human saliva, mayonnaise, corn chip crumbs, and toothpicks stuck in those little holes.

> Someday when the kids are grown . . . I'll be able to see through the car windows. Fingerprints, tongue licks, sneaker footprints will be conspicuous by their absence.

> Someday when the kids are grown . . . we

won't run out of toilet tissue. My wife won't lose her keys. We won't forget to shut the refrigerator door. I won't have to dream up new ways of diverting attention from the gumball machine . . . or have to answer "Daddy, is it a sin that you're driv-ing forty-seven in a thirty-mile-per-hour zone?" . . . or promise to kiss the rabbit goodnight . . . or wait up forever until they get home from dates.

Yes, someday when the kids are grown . . . things are going to be a lot differ-ent. The phone will be strangely silent. The house will be quiet . . . and calm . . . and always clean . . . and very, very empty . . . and we'll spend our time not looking forward to "Someday" but looking back to "Yesterday."[15]

MAKING TIME FOR TEACHABLE MOMENTS

There is a Latin phrase my son picked up when studying in Cambridge, England. It is *carpe diem*, or "seize the day." Take advantage of every opportu-nity to teach, train, and set godly examples for your family. Pray for God to honor the quantity time that you spend with your family. Ask Him to send divine appointments your way. Ask God to help you respond with patience, gentleness and positive instruction when bad things happen. We teach by *being*. Our family sees who we really are by what we say and do.

Teachable moments are those times that you pray for and look for. The nature of a teachable moment is that it has the potential to either tear down or build up. Following are some examples that our family has experienced:

Teachable Moment #1. My daughter and I came home one evening to find water everywhere. Amber was 8 at the time, a very sensitive, caring young child. My wife, Kathy, had left the washer on; it malfunctioned and water was flooding the end of the house. We had just remodeled and water was going through the walls and flooding the downstairs as well. I was in a panic. I couldn't get the water turned off. Water was everywhere and continued to flow. I made desperate calls to reach a plumber but to no avail. Amber was beside herself. I saw fear in her eyes—fear because of the damage to the house and fear that I was going to be very angry with her mother.

I found myself right in the middle of a bona fide "teachable moment." In the middle of all the chaos, with water running everywhere, I stopped and sat down with Amber at the kitchen table to calm her down. I lovingly and calmly took both of her hands into mine, looked straight into her eyes and said, "Amber, everything is going to be fine. I love you. I love your mother. I'm not angry at her. Amber, everything that's getting wet can be replaced. You, your mother and this family are what's most important. Everything will be fine."

I was so proud of myself. I passed the test of seizing the teachable moment this time. So many times I fail, but this time I saw an opportunity to teach and set an example. I had carpet that was damaged, but *more importantly*, I had a child that needed me. I had furniture that may be ruined, but *more importantly*, I had an eternal soul to influence. I had a huge mess and I was upset, but *more importantly*, I had an opportunity to show Christlikeness in a time of trouble.

It is these kinds of teachable moments that children remember during times of adverse circumstances. In setting an example for them, we are training them how they, in turn, will respond in those same kind of situations with their children (our grandchildren). And the cycle continues. If we only exhibit Christlikeness when things go well, what kind of example are we setting for our family?

A family was watching a TV program about a boy searching for the perfect parents, only to discover that his own family really did love him. It seemed like a good opportunity to ask their sweet, but often intolerant, teenage daughter if she ever wanted to find another set of parents. "No, Mom," she answered. "You and Dad are so moody it's like having a different set of parents every day!" 1 Timothy instructs us, "But be thou an example of the believer, in word, in conversation, in charity, in spirit, in faith, in purity" (4:12, KJV). Titus 2:7 tells us, "In everything set them an example by doing what is good."

Teachable Moment #2. Kathy and I were traveling back from Indianapolis, Indiana, to Cleveland, Tennessee, with our two daughters — Amber, who was 7 at the time, and Sylvia, who was 13. What an opportunity for teachable moments!

A few days earlier I had purposefully put some flash cards in the car. The Keyword Learning System has full-color, very creative cartoon-like pictures that depict every book in the Bible and its major theme. Seizing the moment, I challenged the girls to learn every Old Testament book and the major themes of each. In just a few hours, both of my children learned the major themes of every book in the Old Testament.

A few weeks later, I took Amber, my 7-year-old, to a class I teach at Lee University. I stood her in front of 85 college students and asked them to stump her if they could. They couldn't. They asked her to name the themes of Nahum, Zephaniah, Hosea and many others. She knew them all. The girls have since learned all of the New Testament themes and now we continue to quiz each other as we travel back and forth to school or while sitting in restaurants. It also provides a wonderful opportunity for me to explain the significance and meaning behind all of those major themes of each book in the Bible. What glorious teachable moments!

Teachable Moment #3. This is not one from our family archives and I'm not sure it really happened, but the message is noteworthy. Paul Harvey told the story of a little girl who was out in the backyard brushing the dog's teeth. Her father stops by and asks, "What are you doing?" She says, "Well, I'm brushing Scruffy's teeth." She pauses and says to her father, "Don't worry, Dad. I'll put your toothbrush back like I always do."[16] Definitely a teachable moment.

Teachable Moment #4. The following unique teachable moment is shared by Bruce Larson in the article "Summer Vacation." He writes about a family "memory maker":

> I have a great friend down in Montgomery, Alabama, and a few years ago he told me an unforgettable story of a summer vacation he had planned for his wife and children. He was unable to go because of business, but he helped them plan every day of camping trip in the family station wagon from Montgomery all the way to California, up the West Coast, and then back to Montgomery.
>
> He knew their route exactly and the precise time they would be crossing the Great Divide. So, my friend arranged to fly himself out to the nearest airport and hire a car and a driver to take him to a place, which every car must pass. He sat by the side of the road several hours waiting for the sight of that familiar station wagon. When it came into view, he stepped out in the road and put his thumb out to hitchhike a ride with the family who assumed that he was 3,000 miles away.
>
> "Well, Bruce," he said, "someday I'm going to be dead, and when that happens, I want my kids and my wife to say, "You know, Dad was a lot of fun."

Wow, I thought. Here's a man whose whole game plan is to make fun and happiness for his family. It made me wonder what my own family will remember about me. I'm sure they will say, "Well, Dad was a nice guy but he sure worried a lot about putting out the lights and closing the windows and picking up around the house and cutting the grass." But I'd also like them to be able to say that Dad was the guy who made life a lot of fun.[17]

I have three important questions for parents:

1. After all is said and done in your family, can you say that your time was well spent?

2. Have you taken time to make memories for a lifetime?

3. Years from now, how will you be remembered by your family?

A few years ago, the late Senator Paul Tsougas contemplated running for president. During that time, he announced that he was a workaholic. Later, he was diagnosed with cancer. He left his Washington office to return home to do some soul-searching. Afterward, he made a statement that impressed me: "When I get to the end of my life and I'm lying on my death bed, I don't think I'll say, 'Gee, I wish I had spent more time at the office.'"[18]

Arthur Gordon describes how time will either be spent for eternal purposes or lost forever:

When I was around 13 and my brother was
10, Father promised to take us to the circus.
But at lunch, there was a phone call. Some
urgent business required his attention down-
town. My brother and I braced ourselves for
the disappointment. Then we heard him say,
"No, I won't be down. It will have to wait."
When he came back to the table, Mother
smiled and said, "The circus keeps coming
back you know."

"I know," said Father, "but childhood doesn't."[19]

Opportunities to bless our spouses and build
precious memories of a lifetime are usually single-
night engagements. If you are truly seeking a
deeper walk in the spirit, seeking to have a servant's heart, and seeking to live Christlike, you
will bless your family with the best of your life —
your time. That may be the spark that ignites spiritual renewal in your family.

10
Committed to Living and Leaving a Spiritual Heritage

In his seminar *You and Your Family*, Dr. Tim LaHaye shared an interesting chart depicting the legacy of two different men who lived in the 18th century. The first man was an alleged moonshiner named Max Jukes. He never attended church, nor did his wife. The second man was a godly man named Jonathan Edwards. Through his sermons, the Great Awakening was ignited. His wife was a godly woman who shared the same faith.

Of Max Jukes' 1,026 descendants, 300 died prematurely, 100 were sent to prison, 190 were prostitutes, and 100 were town drunks. Of Dr. Edwards' 729 descendants, 300 were preachers, 65 were college professors, 13 were authors, three were congressmen, and one was vice president of the United States.

The Bible gives us insight into the legacy of these two men and why their families evolved the way they did. "Do not be deceived: God cannot be mocked. A man reaps what he sows. The one who sows to please his sinful nature, from that nature will reap destruction; the one who sows to please the Spirit, from the Spirit will reap eternal life" (Galatians 6:7, 8).

Charles Stanley paraphrases it like this: "You reap *what* you sow, you reap *more* than you sow, and you reap *later* than you sow." The value systems and lifestyles in our families today are likely to be manifested in the family relationships of our children and their children.

An incident in the Civil War applies this truth. At the height of the bloodshed an average of 2,000 Union soldiers per week were dying and their bodies being shipped back north to be buried. With so many bodies to be buried, there was a great need for a new cemetery. It was General Montgomery Meigs' responsibility to select the site for the new cemetery. General Meigs' own son had perished in the Shenandoah Valley battle. The general's bitterness led him to select the grounds surrounding the Virginia home of Confederate General Robert E. Lee as the site for the new cemetery. General Lee's home, on the banks of the Potomac, had become the Arlington National Cemetery — the most sacred ground of the Union army. The irony is that so many of the young men killed by General Lee's forces were now buried in his own front yard.

This lesson came home to haunt us in our own parenting roles. Rolf Zetterstein, in the book *Train Up a Child,* writes: "Our deeds, our priorities, our values will come home to rest in our front yards through the lives of our children."[1] A strong commitment to spiritual values will ensure that good

things come home to us. One of the best examples
of this is found in Steve Farrar's book, *Point Man*.
He talks about a man named George McClusky:

> McCluskey was a man who decided to make
> a shrewd investment. As he married and start-
> ed a family, he decided to invest one hour a
> day in prayer. He was concerned that his kids
> might follow Christ and establish their own
> homes where Christ was honored. After a
> time, he decided to expand his prayers to
> include not only his children, but their chil-
> dren and the children after them. Every day
> between 11 a.m. and noon, he would pray for
> the next three generations.
>
> As the years went by, his two daughters com-
> mitted their lives to Christ and married men
> who went into full-time ministry. The two
> couples produced four girls and one boy. Each
> of the girls married a minister and the boy
> became a pastor. The first two children born to
> this generation were both boys. One became a
> minister, but the other chose not to go into full-
> time ministry. He was the first one in four gen-
> erations not to do so. He decided to pursue
> his interest in psychology. After earning his
> doctorate, he wrote a book to parents that
> became a best-seller. He then wrote another
> and another, all best-sellers. Eventually he
> started a radio program that is now heard on
> more than a thousand stations each day. The
> man's name? James Dobson, without doubt

the most influential and significant leader of
the pro-family movement in America. His
ministry is the direct result of the prayers of a
man who lived four generations ago.[2]

A good man leaves an inheritance for his children's
children (Proverbs 13:22).

A GODLY LEGACY *We have an opportunity to do something about the heritage we pass down.*

We will pass down a heritage to the next generation. The only question is, what kind of heritage?"
Otis Ledbetter, in his book *The Heritage,* says: "A heritage is the spiritual, emotional, and social legacy
that is passed from parent to child — good or bad."[3]

The Bible addresses the reality of generational
continuity. Many of our actions, words, deeds,
prayers and lifestyles yield their harvest in the lives
of our children, our grandchildren and future generations. We are all the products of other people.
The fact is that the values, habits and lifestyles of
our ancestors have had a significant influence on
our own lives.

Billy Graham gave this insight about a family
legacy: "Parents should first cultivate their souls
that in turn they may cultivate the souls of their
children."[4] As husbands, wives, dads and moms
seek God for a more intimate relationship with
Him, they automatically grow closer to their
spouses and children. This type of intimate relationship with God develops a lifestyle that ensures
a spiritual legacy. I think it would be very helpful

for us to look again at Deuteronomy 6:6, 7: "These commandments that I give you today are to be upon your hearts. Impress them on your children." That's the formula for future generations to receive godly heritage.

A positive, godly and affirming environment has a greater chance of yielding healthier children—spiritually, emotionally and socially. On the flip side, a family filled with negative, ungodly attributes yields devastating results. Research conducted with students who were chosen for *Who's Who Among American High School Students* produced some interesting results. The survey asked students whether they lived in happy or unhappy homes and examined the relationship between home life and behavior. They found that teens from unhappy homes are . . .

- Nearly five times more likely to smoke

- Twice as likely to drink to the point of being drunk

- More likely to commit suicide (18 percent, compared to 2 percent of teens from happy homes)

- More likely to engage in premarital sex (46 percent compared to 20 percent)

- More likely to have sex with a stranger (44 percent compared to 30 percent)[5]

Negative experiences in unhappy homes are perpetuated for generations to come. Malachi gives a

somber warning about our responsibility to the
next generation. "He will turn the hearts of the
fathers to their children, and the hearts of the children to their fathers; or else I will come and strike
the land with a curse" (4:6).

On the other hand, God gives precious promises
to those who remain faithful:

> We will not hide them from their children;
> we will tell the next generation the praise-
> worthy deeds of the Lord, his power, and the
> wonders he has done. He decreed statutes
> for Jacob and established the law in Israel,
> which he commanded our forefathers to
> teach their children, so the next generation
> would know them, even the children yet to
> be born, and they in turn would tell their
> children. Then they would put their trust in
> God and would not forget his deeds but
> would keep his commands (Psalm 78:4-7).

The words we speak, the services we render and
the love we show can bless our sons, daughters and
families for generations to come.

Commitment – devoted, Vulnerable,
Takes Time
Hard work
Sacrifice

COMMITMENT IS THE KEY

Responsibility The story is told of a man who became so
Selfish depressed his wife thought he was going to die. He
Accountability went into his bedroom, pulled the drapes and laid
Inconvenience on his bed in a fetal position. His wife pleaded with
him to go to the doctor, but he refused. Finally, in

We are in the age of Non-commitment; if it feels good, just do it.

desperation, the wife decided she would speak to the doctor. When she explained all her husband's symptoms to the doctor, he gave her specific instructions. She was to prepare the nicest breakfast that she had ever prepared: squeeze fresh orange juice, make homemade cinnamon rolls, scramble fresh eggs, fry bacon and home fries—anything his heart desired. She was then to take him for a walk in the neighborhood, bring him back home and give him a foot massage. At noon she was instructed to prepare his favorite lunch with a vase of fresh flowers and homemade bread. Then she was to take him for another walk, bring him home and give him a back massage. In the evening, the doctor instructed her to prepare a candlelight dinner, complete with soft music and his favorite homemade dessert. After that, he was to go for another walk, brought back in and given a head massage. The doctor instructed her to do that every day for about three weeks, and her husband should be fine. When the wife went back home, her husband asked what the doctor said. Her reply was, "The doctor said you're going to die." Not quite the same message. The commitment to *live* and *leave* a godly legacy requires a commitment that stands regardless of the circumstances, temptations and trials.

In seeking to build strong families, we may learn from the findings of research that identifies common ingredients of a healthy home. One list came from a summary review of research studies conducted over recent decades. A second list came from a recent study of 3,000 strong families in South America,

Switzerland, Austria, Germany, South Africa, and the United States. A third list came from interviews by Jeane Westin, who authored *The Coming Parent Revolution*. Robert Hamrin condensed these surveys and revealed that one strong family element was cited in all three lists, while five other elements were cited in two of three lists. These six characteristics are key factors to a strong family:

1. The family has a spiritual commitment (all three lists).

2. Members love each other, and the family is a unit.

3. Family members spend time together.

4. Good communication exists between family members.

5. Ability to solve problems in crisis is common.

6. Family members express appreciation to each other.[6]

The one answer that made all three lists was *spiritual commitment in the family*. That's the foundation for spiritual renewal! In the face of pressure from all sides, the home is where lifelong values are formed. In his book, *Home! Where Life Makes Up It's Mind*, Chuck Swindoll writes:

> Whatever else may be said about the home, it is the bottom line of life, the anvil upon which attitudes and convictions are hammered out.

It is the place where life's bills come due, the single most influential force in our earthly existence. No price tag can adequately reflect its value. No gauge can measure its ultimate influence—for good or ill. It is at home, among family members, that we come to terms with circumstances. It is here life makes up its mind.[7]

The home is actually the church in miniature and the father is the appointed pastor of his own home. Parents are the spiritual leaders in the family. Too many parents wash their hands of the responsibility to provide spiritual training. They expect, even demand, that the church fulfill that responsibility. It is not the pastor, youth pastor, children's pastor or even the Sunday school teacher's responsibilities. It is *our* responsibility as parents. As Deuteronomy points out:

These commandments that I give *you* today are to be upon your hearts. Impress them on your children. (6:6, italics added).

We need to commit to live in obedience to this command, because obedience ushers in spiritual renewal.

A few days ago, someone told me about a particular denomination that was reluctant to develop a Sunday school ministry because it was concerned that parents would somehow absolve themselves of their responsibility to teach and train their children.

As a Christian educator for more than 25 years, I see this scene played out in families every day. Churches should help, but parents are primarily responsible for the spiritual training of their children. Every Christian dad and mom should petition God for help as they fulfill this God-given role.

Parents provide training in many ways. An important means of training is the example they set. Someone once remarked that Amish children never speak with anger and malice. In reply, the question was asked: "Well, have you ever seen an Amish parent speak with anger and malice?"

Our children are like sponges absorbing everything they see and hear. Parents can shout one thing from the housetops, but if they live something else, their children don't buy it. As the old adage says, "Our actions speak so loud our kids can't hear a word we say." We can say that attending church, praying and reading the Bible are important, but children are not convinced by words without deeds. We can tell them that serving others is Christlike, but they need to see us serving others. If they see us preoccupied with financial gain, recreational activities and materialistic pursuits, they may question our values.

People spend time and money on the things they truly value. We need take seriously our level of commitment to live and leave a spiritual legacy. Commitment is like the roof on a house—it covers everything else. Commitment seals our dedication to our marriage and our family when we resolve to do the following:

- Keep our family centered on God.

- Be obedient to our role and responsibility in marriage and family.

- Pray for and with our family.

- Nourish our family with the Word of God.

- Love, forgive and serve our spouse and children.

- Let our words express appreciation and affirmation.

- Give our spouse and children the very best of our time and attention.

Strong, spiritual families do not happen by accident. Let us commit to live the words of Joshua: "As for me and my house, we will serve the Lord" (Joshua 24:15, KJV).

The Cornerstone

Most family specialists believe that we must put our marriage first and then our family. One of the best ways for couples to love their kids is to love each other.

> It is vitally important that children see mom and dad "prioritize" the marriage relationship as the first of God's ordained human relationships. Children feel secure as they see a strong level of intimacy between their parents. An intimate foundation in marriage also

> allows children the freedom to grow up. To have a healthy marriage and family, children must sense that mom and dad love each other and are committed to one another.[8]

Couples should beware of the "greener grass syndrome." It is Satan's job to convince husbands and wives that they would be better off with someone else. Harvard sociologist Armand Nichol III contends that "divorce is not a solution, but an exchange of problems."[9] I would like to point out two little-known facts about the grass on the other side of the fence.

First you still have to mow it. Every relationship takes effort, love and attention. Second, it is likely that the grass is greener on the other side of the fence because there is a septic tank under it. Satan can make anything look enticing when in reality, evil and sin lurk beneath the surface.

Maybe you've heard the expression, "Jumping out of the frying pan into the fire." Actually couples shouldn't be living in a frying pan in the first place. God doesn't intend for us to live in turmoil. We can turn down the heat in the pan, but jumping out is not the answer. The success rate for second marriages is not very promising. Of all second marriages, 60-70% do not work out. To put it plainly, God hates divorce:

> Another thing you do: You flood the Lord's altar with tears. You weep and wail because he no longer pays attention to your offerings or accepts them with pleasure from your

hands. You ask, "Why?" It is because the Lord is acting as the witness between you and the wife of your youth, because you have broken faith with her, though she is your partner, the wife of your marriage covenant. Has not the Lord made them one? In flesh and spirit they are his. And why one? Because he was seeking godly offspring. So guard yourself in your spirit, and do not break faith with the wife of your youth. "I hate divorce," says the Lord God of Israel, "and I hate a man's covering himself with violence as well as with his garment," says the Lord Almighty. So guard yourself in your spirit, and do not break faith (Malachi 2:13-16).

There are reasons why God hates divorce so much. He knows it destroys oneness in marriage as He planned it. He also knows it causes hate, strife and dysfunction in families, which are disastrous to the children involved.

In *One House at a Time*, Dennis Rainey outlines the devastation divorce has on the family:

- What makes a child four times more likely to commit a violent crime?

- What increases the likelihood of a child's living in poverty, dropping out of school, and becoming a juvenile delinquent?

- What increases the probability of a child's abusing alcohol, taking drugs, becoming sexually promiscuous, and committing suicide?

- What cripples hundreds of thousands of young people when they marry and creates fear, insecurity, and a higher likelihood that their marriages will not last a lifetime?

It's divorce, divorce, divorce. And divorce is killing both America and the church. Broken promises . . . mistrust . . . instability . . . shattered people. Divorce has created a national disaster. An enemy.

Just like a grenade exploding in a crowded room, the white-hot twisted shrapnel of divorce maims all participants—children and adults. Everyone bleeds. Americans are quick to walk the aisle—and also quick to run away when the marriage gets rough.[10]

Commitment to marriage demands tenacity and perseverance. More couples need the commitment of J.L. and Hilda Simpson: "September 9, 1995, made us 46 years together. I was 15 and J.L. was 17 when we married. We are now 61 and 63. We could have divorced dozens of times, but because we love each other deeply, and because God hates divorce, we didn't want to bring the curse of divorce into our family, so we didn't."[11]

Even in the heat of conflict and hurt, never let the word *divorce* slip through your lips. For the sake of our marriage and children, we must keep our marriage vows. Even our children's marriages will be impacted by our commitment to marriage. The Word of God speaks to issues of perseverance in the marriage relationship: "For this reason a man will leave his father and mother and be united to his wife, and they will become one flesh"(Genesis 2:24).

H. Norman Wright puts it this way: "The Bible's view of marriage is the *total* commitment of the total person for the total life."[12]

Committed to a Plan

In educational circles, I quite often hear about teaching objectives. Whether you call them goals, aims or objectives, the point is that we need to know where we are going. I've heard it said many times, "If you aim at nothing, you will hit it every time."

A prominent businessman once told Howard Hendricks that his company was spending thousands of dollars in planning for the direction of the firm's progress. The same man had failed to spend one hour thinking about the focus of his family's future. Realizing this omission, he took his wife to a motel for a weekend. There they prayed, discussed and planned what they were aiming for in their family.[13]

Marriages and families are worth the time we spend planning and casting a vision for their future. The reality is that many of us try to build our families with no particular objectives or strategies in mind. It's like the airplane pilot who came over the intercom and announced to his passengers, "Ladies and gentlemen, I'm afraid that we are lost, but don't worry; we're making great time." Paul writes, "Let every man take heed *how* he buildeth" (1 Corinthians 3:10, KJV).

Family Staff Meetings

Planning, developing and maintaining a growth plan for marriage and family will require commitment. Kathy and I have gleaned some excellent insights about planning from our experience with "Intimate Life Ministries." Two practical tools are Marriage Staff meetings and Family Staff meetings. No successful business would dare operate without regular staff meetings. Why should marriage and the family be any different? Here are some guidelines for a marriage or family staff meeting:

1. *Have a set time.* Don't leave it to chance. Put it on your calendar and in all planners of family members. Make it a standing appointment for the same time each week.

2. *Make that scheduled time sacred.* Don't cancel it or reschedule it if at all possible. Give it as much a priority as any other appointment on your calendar. (Actually very few things would be more important.) Protect this appointed time from interruption. Let the phone take messages and turn off the TV.

3. *Make a list of agenda items in writing.* Talk about schedules, chores, family devotions, needs, problems, goals, family events, and so forth.

4. *Listen as much as you speak.* The Bible tells us to be "quick to listen and slow to speak" (see James 1:19).

5. *Discuss family goals.* From week to week monitor their progress. Goals could be relational, financial, personal or otherwise.

6. *Share words of appreciation and affirmation.* Let each family member express their appreciation for other family members. (In a Marriage Staff meeting, more intimate words of appreciation and affirmation are encouraged.)[14]

We need to have a vision for our family. Then we must commit our energy, time, devotion and prayer to making it happen.

Helen Keller was once asked, "Is there anything worse than being blind?" She replied, "Yes. The most pathetic person in the whole world is someone who has sight but has no vision."

Proverbs 29:18 tells us, "Where there is no vision, the people perish"(KJV). Ron Rand added to that verse in what he calls the "Rand Revised Version": "Without a vision the people perish, and without a plan, the vision perishes."[15] The level of our commitment to our family will be measured by the time and attention we give it.

"Burn the Ships"

You must decide what kind of commitment *you* are willing to make in order to *live* and *leave* a strong spiritual legacy.

Hernando Cortes had an ambitious plan. He decided to lead an expedition to capture the land of Mexico and all of its vast treasures. The Spanish governor was so elated that he gave Cortes 11 ships and 700 men to complete the mission. Cortes, however, did not reveal his total plan to the governor.

In the spring of 1819, after a long voyage, Cortes and his ships landed in Veracruz, Mexico. After unloading the ships, Cortes implemented the rest of his diabolical plan.

As his men marched inland, they looked back only to see all their ships on fire. Had the enemy set them on fire? No, Cortes himself had his own ships burned. He was saying to his men, "We're committed — totally committed. You either win the battle, or you're dead because there is no going back." We must be totally committed.

We cannot pass on to our children what we do not possess ourselves. The late Ray Stedman was right on target when he said, "We can't expect our children to be changed unless something has changed us," and that "we can only communicate what we ourselves have discovered." He declared, "We must start with ourselves. And then we are responsible to pass on to our children what we have been taught and have learned and discovered in our own experience."[16] As we get closer to God, we automatically get closer to our family. Our intimate relationship with God will be reflected in our attitudes and actions.

God is anxiously awaiting you to seek a fresh encounter with Him in your personal life and in your family. He will honor your diligence with a spiritual renewal in your home like you've never seen before.

Notes

CHAPTER 1

[1]Lamar Vest, *Spiritual Renewal* (Cleveland, TN: Pathway Press, 1988) 22-23.

[2]Warren Wiersbe, *Be Mature* (Wheaton, IL: Victor Books, 1978) 13.

[3]Ray Guarandi, *Back to the Family* (New York: Villard, 1990) 102.

[4]William and Michael Mitchell, *Building Strong Families* (Nashville, TN: Broadman and Holman Publishers, 1997) 11.

[5]Howard Hendricks, *Heaven Help the Home* (Wheaton, IL: Victor Books, 1974) 12.

[6]Steve Farrar, *Point Man* (Portland, OR: Multnomah, 1990) 17-18.

[7]Vest 14.

[8]Hendricks 87-88.

CHAPTER 2

[1]*Intimate Life Ministries Newsletter*, 7.8 (Aug. 1997): 1.

[2]John Maxwell, *Breakthrough Parenting* (Colorado Springs, CO: Focus on the Family Publishing, 1996) 121-22.

[3]Maxwell 122.

[4]Dennis Rainey, *One Home at a Time* (Colorado Springs, CO: Focus on the Family Publishing, 1997) 58.

[5]Rainey 63-64.

[6]Adrian Rodgers, *Ten Secrets for a Successful Family* (Wheaton, IL: Crossway Books, 1996) 45.

[7]Rodgers 45-46.

[8]Howard Hendricks, *Heaven Help the Home* (Wheaton, IL: Victor Books, 1974) 12.

[9]Josh McDowell, *How to Help Your Child Say No to Sexual Pressure* (Waco, TX: Word, Inc., 1987) 101.

CHAPTER 3

[1]Dennis Rainey, *One Home at a Time* (Colorado Springs, CO: Focus on the Family Publishing, 1997) 167-68.

[2]Rainey 168.

[3]Steve Farrar, *Point Man* (Portland, OR: Multnomah Press, 1990) 135.

[4]Farrar 137.

[5]James Dobson, *Love for a Lifetime* (Sisters, OR: Multnomah Press, 1993) 53-54.

[6]Intimate Life Ministries, "Experiencing God in Marriage, Family and the Church," *A Handbook for*

Reclaiming Marriage and Family as Divine Relationships (Austin, TX: Intimacy Press, 1995) 31.

[7]E. Glenn Wagner, *Strategies for a Successful Marriage* (Colorado Springs, CO: Navpress, 1994) 106.

[8]Rainey 86.

[9]Ray Guarandi, *Back to the Family* (New York: Villard, 1990) 102.

[10]Joe White, *Orphans at Home* (Phoenix: Questar, 1988) 223-24.

[11]Charles Stanley, *How to Keep Your Kids on Your Team* (Nashville, TN: Oliver Nelson Publishers, 1986) 104.

[12]John Maxwell, "Getting to Know God With Your Children," online, Focus on the Family, Internet, 1995, available HTTP:www.family.org

[13]Bill Carmichael, *7 Habits of a Happy Home* (Wheaton, IL: Tyndale House Publishers, 1997) 237.

[14]Bill Hylels, *Too Busy Not to Pray* (Downers Grove, IL: Intervarsity Press, 1988) 9.

[15]J.C. Ryle, *A Call to Prayer* (Grand Rapids: Baker Book House, 1979) 35.

[16]C.H. Spurgeon, "Prayer — The Forerunner of Mercy," *New Park Street Pulpit*, vol. 3 (1858; Pasadena, TX: Pilgrim Publications, 1981) 251.

CHAPTER 4

[1]Robert Summer, "Treasuring God's Word," *Our Daily Bread*, Oct. 5, 1988.

[2]John Blanchard, *How to Enjoy Your Bible* (Colchester, England: Evangelical Press, 1984) 104.

[3]Donald S. Whitney, *Spiritual Disciples for the Christian Life* (Colorado Springs, CO: Navpress, 1991) 40-41.

[4]Whitney 44

[5]George Mueller, *Spiritual Secrets of George Mueller*, ed. Roger Stear (Wheaton, IL: Harold Shaw Publishers, 1985) 60-62.

[6]Thomas Manton, *The Works of Thomas Manton* (Worthington, PA: Maranatha Publications, n.d.) 272-73.

[7]Avery T. Willis Jr., *Master Life* (Nashville: Broadman & Holman Publishers, 1998) 20.

[8]James S. Hewett, *Illustrations Unlimited* (Wheaton, IL: Tyndale House Publishers, Inc., 1988) 354.

[9]"How We Respond to the Word of God," *Intimate Life Training Manual,* handout #6, Leadership Institute (Austin, TX: Intimate Life Ministries, n.d.).

[10]Edgar Dale, *Audiovisual Methods in Teaching* (New York: Holt, Rinehart and Winston, 1969) 108.

CHAPTER 5

[1]Resource, online, Internet, Sept./Oct. 1992, available HTTP:www.thurmanillustrations.com

[2]Ron Gilbert, ed., *Bits & Pieces* (Fairfield, NJ: The Economic Press, Inc., 25 June 1992).

[3]Arthur F. Leneham, compiler and ed., *The Best of Bits and Pieces* (Fairfield, NJ: The Economic Press, Inc., 1994) 73.

[4]*Draper's Book of Quotations for the Christian World* (Wheaton, IL: Tyndale House Publishing, 1992) 235.

[5]Ron Hutchcraft, *Start Your Trip With a Full Tank* (Grand Rapids: Baker Books, 1996) 169.

[6]Intimate Life Ministries, "Experiencing God in Marriage, Family and the Church," *A Handbook for Reclaiming Marriage and Family as Divine Relationships* (Austin, TX: Intimacy Press, 1995) 143.

[7]Tim Kimmel, *Little House on the Freeway* (Portland, OR: Multnomah Press, 1987) 163.

[8]William and Nancie Carmichael, *601 Quotes About Marriage and Family* (Wheaton, IL: Tyndale House Publishers, Inc., 1998) 280-81.

[9]Phillip Yancey, *Leadership* (Carol Stream, IL: Christianity Today, Inc, Fall 1995) 41.

[10]Richard Foster, *Celebration of Discipline* (San Francisco, CA: Harper and Rowe, 1978) 110.

[11]Donald S. Whitney, *Spiritual Disciplines for the Christian Life* (Colorado Springs, CO: Navpress, 1991) 115.

[12]Gary Chapman, *Five Signs of a Functional Family* (Chicago: Northfield Publishing, 1997) 29.

CHAPTER 6

[1]E. Glenn Wagner, *Strategies for a Successful Marriage* (Colorado Springs, CO: Navpress, 1994) 66.

[2]David Ferguson, *The Great Commandment Principle* (Wheaton, IL: Tyndale House Publishers, Inc., 1998) 43-60.

[3]Max and Vivian Rice, "How to Know When You Are Really in Love," *Families – Practical Advice From More Than 50 Experts*, ed. Jenny Jenkins (Chicago: Moody Press, 1995) 18.

[4]Ron Phillips, *Home Improvement* (Cleveland, TN: Pathway Press, 1996) 23.

[5]Henry Overstreet, *The Nature Mind* (New York: Norton Publishers, 1969) 105.

[6]Rice 16-24.

[7]Gary Chapman, *Five Signs of a Functional Family* (Chicago: Northfield Publishers, 1997) 90-91.

[8]Alice Gray, *More Stories From the Heart* (Sisters, OR: Multnomah Publishers, Inc., 1997) 154.

[9]William and Nancie Carmichael, *601 Quotes About Marriage and Family* (Wheaton, IL: Tyndale House Publishers, Inc., 1998) 94, 95.

[10]Adrian Rodgers, *Ten Secrets for a Successful Family* (Wheaton, IL: Crossway Books, 1996) 115.

[11]Arthur F. Leneham, compiler and ed., *The Best of Bits and Pieces* (Fairfield, NJ: The Economic Press, Inc., 1994) 194.

CHAPTER 7

[1]Tim Kimmel, *Little House on the Freeway* (Portland, OR: Multnomah Press, 1987) 60-61.

[2]E. Glen Wagner, *Strategies for a Successful Marriage* (Colorado Springs, CO: Navpress, 1994) 16.

[3]Intimate Life Ministries, "Experiencing God in Marriage, Family and the Church," *A Handbook for Reclaiming Marriage and Family as Divine Relationships* (Austin, TX: Intimacy Press, 1995) 206.

[4]Ron Gilbert, *More of . . . The Best of Bits and Pieces* (Fairfield, NJ: The Economic Press, Inc., 1997) 74.

[5]Jay Adams, *More Than Redemption* (Phillipsburg, NJ: Presbyterian and Reformed Publishers Co., 1979) 228.

[6]Mike Yorkey, compiler and ed., *The Christian Family Answer Book* (Wheaton, IL: Victor Books, 1996) 221.

CHAPTER 8

[1]Paul Walker, "The Greatest Power in All the World," *Church of God Evangel*, Oct. 1998.

[2]Jack Canfield and Mark Victor Hansen, *Chicken Soup for the Soul 101: Stories to Open the Heart and Rekindle the Spirit* (Deerfield Beach, FL: Health Communications, Inc., 1993) 43-44.

[3]Robert E. Fisher, *Quick to Listen, Slow to Speak* (Wheaton, IL: Tyndale House Publishers, 1987) 152.

[4]William and Nancie Carmichael, *601 Quotes About Marriage and Family* (Wheaton, IL: Tyndale House Publishers, Inc., 1998) 288.

[5]George Rekers, ed., *Family Building* (Ventura, CA: Regal Books, 1985) 88.

[6]Arthur F. Leneham, compiler and ed., *The Best of Bits and Pieces* (Fairfield, NJ: The Economic Press, Inc., 1994) 143.

[7]Jack Cranfield, *Chicken Soup for the Soul* (Deerfield Beach, FL: Health Communications, Inc., 1993) n. pag.

[8]Jerry and Jack Schreur Gospel Communications Internet article summary. International Updates and Information. Better Families: A Simple Magic of Affirmation. online, Online Christian Resources, Internet, available: HTTP:www .gospelcom.net/

[9]William and Nancie Carmichael, *601 Quotes*

About Marriage and Family (Wheaton, IL: Tyndale House Publishers, Inc., 1998) 240.

CHAPTER 9

[1]Kathy Seals, personal E-mail.

[2]Ken and Betty Gangel, *Your Family – Biblical Solutions for Raising Children* (Gresham, OR: Vision House Publishing, 1995) 129-30.

[3]William Mitchell and Michael Mitchell, *Building Strong Families* (Nashville, TN: Broadman and Holman Publishers, 1997) 18.

[4]Steve Farrar, *Standing Tall* (Sisters, OR: Multnomah Press, 1994) 224.

[5]Gary Bauer, *Our Journey Home* (Dallas: Word Publishing, 1992) 134-35.

[6]Shelley McDermid, *Cleveland Daily Banner*, 27 Jan. 1999.

[7]Josh McDowell, "Love Is Spelled TIME," *Families – Practical Advice From More Than 50 Experts*, ed. Jerry Jenkins, (Chicago: Moody Press, 1995) 62.

[8]Erma Bombeck, *Family – The Ties That Bind . . . and Gag!* (New York: Faucett, 1988) 2.

[9]Cathy Trost and Ellen Gzrech, "What Happened When Five Families Stopped Watching TV," *Good Housekeeping Magazine*, Aug. 1979, n. pag.

[10]Gloria Gaither and Shirley Dobson, *Let's Make a Memory* (Dallas: Word Publishing, 1994) 204.

[11]J. Otis Ledbetter and Tim Smith, *Heritage Builders, Family Traditions* (Colorado Springs, CO: Victor Publishing, 1998) 32.

[12]Ron Clarkson, *Introducing the Spiritual Side of Parenting* (Colorado Springs, CO: Lion Publishing, 1998) 62.

[13]Edith Schaeffer, *What Is Family?* (Old Tappan, NJ: Fleming H. Revell, 1975) 189.

[14]Stephen R. Covey, *The 7 Habits of Highly Effective Families* (New York: Golden Books, 1997) 280.

[15]William and Nancie Carmichael, *601 Quotes About Marriage and Family* (Wheaton, IL: Tyndale House Publishers, Inc., 1998) 308-09.

[16]*Paul Harvey News*, March 1988.

[17]Alice Gray, *Stories From the Heart* (Sisters, OR: Multnomah Publishers, 1996) 173.

[18]Clarkson 196.

[19]William and Nancie Carmichael, *601 Quotes About Marriage and Family* (Wheaton, IL: Tyndale House Publishers, Inc., 1998) 310.

CHAPTER 10

[1]Rolf Zetterstein, *Train Up a Child* (Wheaton, IL: Tyndale House Publishers, Inc., 1991) 10.

[2]Steve Farrar, *Point Man* (Portland, OR: Multnomah, 1990) 154-55.

[3]J. Otis Ledbetter and Kurt Bruner, *The Heritage* (Colorado Springs, CO: Victor Publishing, 1996) 27.

[4]Jean Fleming, *A Mother's Heart* (Colorado Springs, CO: Navpress, 1987) 65.

[5]William Mitchell and Michael Mitchell, *Building Strong Families* (Nashville, TN: Broadman and Holman Publishers, 1997) 145.

[6]Robert Hamrin, *Straight Talk From a Dad's Heart* (Nashville, TN: Nelson Publishers, 1993) 238.

[7]Charles R. Swindoll, *Home: Where Life Makes Up Its Mind* (Portland, OR: Multnomah, 1997) 5.

[8]Intimate Life Ministries, "Experiencing God in Marriage, Family and the Church," *A Handbook for Reclaiming Marriage and Family as Divine Relationships* (Austin, TX: Intimacy Press, 1995) 217.

[9]Quoted in Wallerstein and Blakeslee, *Second Chances*, xxi.

[10]Dennis Rainey, *One Home at a Time* (Colorado Springs, CO: Focus on the Family Publishing, 1997) 79-80.

[11]Rainey 85.

[12]H. Norman Wright, *Communications: Key to Your Marriage — Group Study Guide* (Gospel Light, 1975).

[13]Howard Hendricks, *Heaven Help the Home* (Wheaton, IL: Victor Books, 1974) 133.

[14]Intimate Life Ministries, "Experiencing God in Marriage, Family and the Church," *A Handbook for Reclaiming Marriage and Family as Divine Relationships* (Austin, TX: Intimacy Press, 1995) 203-05.

[15]Ron Rand, *For Fathers Who Aren't in Heaven* (Ventura, CA: Regal Books, 1986) 17.

[16]Ray Stedman, "Life: The Teacher," online, Internet, 18 Feb. 1973, available: HTTP:www.pbc .org/dplstedman/guidelines/3024.html